The Question of Silence

The Question of Silence

A Para-biography

G. N. Devy

Orient BlackSwan

THE QUESTION OF SILENCE: A PARA-BIOGRAPHY

ORIENT BLACKSWAN PRIVATE LIMITED

Registered Office
3-6-752 Himayatnagar, Hyderabad 500 029, Telangana, India
e-mail: centraloffice@orientblackswan.com

Other Offices
Bengaluru, Bhopal, Chennai, Guwahati,
Hyderabad, Jaipur, Kolkata, Lucknow, Mumbai,
New Delhi, Noida, Patna, Visakhapatnam

First published by Orient Blackswan Private Limited 2019

030277

ISBN 978-93-5287-767-6

Typeset in
Adobe Jenson Pro 12/14.5
by Le Studio Graphique, Gurgaon 122 001

Printed in India at
Akash Press, Delhi

Published by
Orient Blackswan Private Limited
3-6-752, Himayatnagar, Hyderabad 500 029, Telangana, India
e-mail: info@orientblackswan.com

For
Rashmi and Ishaan

Contents

REFLECTIONS

Publishers' Acknowledgements

For granting permission to use copyrighted material in this volume, the publishers would like to thank the following:

Rita Kothari, and Oxford University Press, for a segment in 'Silence on the Horizon', originally published in the essay 'Changing Script' by G. N. Devy, in *A Multilingual Nation: Translation and Language Dynamic in India*, edited by Rita Kothari (New Delhi: Oxford University Press, 2018).

Rashmi Poddar, Jnanapravaha Mumbai, for 'Language Diversity', a lecture by G. N. Devy at Jnanapravaha Mumbai, 22 November 2010; and Rupalee Burke, for her transcription of the lecture.

Rupalee Burke, for her transcription of 'Aesthetics for our Time', the Ashok Ranade Memorial Lecture by G. N. Devy at National Centre for Performing Arts, Mumbai, 10 December 2013.

Gulan Kripalani, Citizens for Peace, for 'Language, Culture, Tribal Struggles and Indian Democracy', a conversation with Dilip D'Souza, G. N. Devy and S. Parasuraman at PeaceTalks, Mumbai, 21 January 2011.

Chitra Padmanabhan, and *The Hindu*, for 'Multilingualism and Cultural Pluralism', originally published as 'We are talking more using fewer words', in *The Hindu*, 3 September 2013.

Kiran Singh, for 'More Intuitive, Less Rational', an interview of G. N. Devy on 25 November 2014.

Yagnesh Dave, for 'And We Come to a Standstill', originally published in Gujarati as '*Ganesh Devy Sathe Vartalap*' [A Conversation with Ganesh Devy], in two parts, in the Gujarati periodical *Navneet Samarpan* (April 2014: 52–74 and May 2014: 46–84); and Rupalee Burke, for the English translation.

Rossella Ciocca, and *Anglistica AION*, for 'Beyond Cultural Aphasia', originally published as 'Beyond Cultural Aphasia: A Conversation with Ganesh Devy on Indian Adivasis', in *Anglistica AION* 19(1): 25–35, 2015.

Shirley Chew, and *Moving Worlds*, for 'Baroda', originally published as 'Baroda: What a City!', in 'Postcolonial Cities: South Asia', *Moving Worlds: A Journal of Transcultural Writings* 13(2): 24–34, 2013.

Acknowledgements

I am beholden to Shiv Visvanathan and Vidya Rao for commenting on an earlier larger and a more chaotic version of the text. Their criticism helped me in reducing it to a half of its original so as to make it less inaccessible.

If it is not misunderstood as a sign of senility, I would like to mention Dastak. She joined my family when she was a two-week-old pup. For years together she was an inalienable part of my life. In March 2016, Surekha and I decided to give up our city of residence in Gujarat, where we had lived for the previous four decades, and to move south. The month of March that year was unusually hot. Dastak could not have withstood it. And she did not. We arrived in our new town of residence after having to bury her on the way in one of the Sahyadri hills. Her absence led me to think of silence more gravely than ever before. She would have wordlessly understood most of my thoughts compressed in these pages. I think of her.

My life has been a series of unfinished conversations. I think of all those now eternally silenced friends and mentors whose conversations have made me what I am: Suresh Joshi, Robert Welch, Arun Kolatkar, Dilip Chitre, Vijay Tendulkar, Narayanbhai Desai, Mahasweta Devi, Geoffrey Davis, and

U. R. Ananthamurthy. Alas, I cannot convey my gratitude to them.

Readers not familiar with the various cultural struggles I have undertaken at different stages in my life and the entire saga of the vast languages survey will no doubt find this work chaotic and a 'dark text'. I do not think any publisher would have thought of publishing it in the present form, despite my having written or edited close to some eighty books. I thank Vidya Rao and Orient BlackSwan for being indulgent to me in taking the risk of bringing out this text. The manuscript I had imagined would be this book and the text as it is now are as different as a block of coal and a diamond. The credit for the transformation goes to Moyna Mazumdar who brought her exceptionally intuitive skills of copy-editing to my help. I thank her.

1 The Question of Silence

1

As I write this in 2016, I am thinking of 1982, Netherlands and Marleen Gorris. Gorris, accidently pushed into directing a film, makes her debut. Cox Habbema is brought in to play the role of a court psychologist. Her challenge is to fathom why three complete strangers got together to murder a clothes-boutique proprietor. These three women—an office assistant, a housewife and a waitress—have been the most unlikely of killers. The man they have killed is unknown to them. Was it their suppressed rage against patriarchy? Was it their existential angst as in Albert Camus' *Outsider*? The film follows the process of investigation, criminal and psychological. It is clear that the crime is committed by them. The more important part of the film is what they hold back in their shared silence. Gorris' controversial debut film, which has become an iconic feminist classic, was titled *A Question of Silence*. The genius of Gorris has since then been recognised worldwide as being disturbingly visionary. The question she raised through her film was: Aren't the stories of the three strange women really a single and universal narrative? The plot does not provide any answers. Having raised the question, it remains silent.

2

... I gave commands
Then all smiles stopped together. There she stands
As if alive ...

This is how the protagonist of Robert Browning's dramatic 1842 monologue *My Last Duchess* describes the silence he orders for the gorgeous duchess. Drawn on probably the fifth Duke of Ferrara in sixteenth-century Italy, he considers honour to be above love. It is his honour that is to be protected by forcing her into an eternal silence. It is the same order of silence that Ms. Benade of Vijay Tendulkar's *Silence! The Court is in Session* has to face, though the twentieth-century context of Tendulkar's Marathi play could not have featured a medieval Italian torture-trap as in Browning's chilling poem.

Yet, at the root of the horror in their respective portrayals, the question is essentially the same.

3

Questions come to us from many quarters. They may spring up in challenge to the practices of patriarchy, the insensitivity of the State, the ruthlessness of the market, the insidiousness of corporate capital, the mindless violence of terrorists, the callousness of class and caste, the inane indifference of satiated consumers to injustice and discrimination, or the sham spirituality and orthodoxies dominated by dogma. Questions keep arising, agitating the mind, from embattled life stories and sites of victimhood. At their most intense, most fierce forms they can be articulated in a language of silence alone, in distrust, agony and contempt.

Silence, too, comes to us from many directions. It comes with compassion, with love, with trust. It comes from wonder, admiration and ecstasy. It comes from peace, transformation and dissolution. It can come from loss, pain and penitence. It can come from tyranny, hegemony, totalitarian and oppressive power.

4

The question of silence, despite the obvious mutual negation of the two terms, needs consideration now as never before. The question is no longer limited to any particular ethnic group, nation, gender, language and culture, or a given faith, philosophy and ideology. It now starkly faces us as our collective destiny on several fronts.

The most widely perceived element of silence is that which the dominated peoples, genders, tongues, cultures and nations have to live with. Post-colonial and post-industrial societies have had to internalise silence in innumerable ways in all aspects of life, including the forms of knowledge imposed on them, the architecture of habitats and urban designs that have entrapped them, the truncated ecologies they are marooned in, the capital-lag and the energy deficits they live with, and finally the lowering of their self-esteem in their own eyes. The silence imposed by the dominant is a fallout of the many known and as-yet-unstated histories of domination. Within these germinate fantasies of subversion, desires of resistance, negation of selfhood and suppression of memory.

5

There is another aspect of silence threatening us. That is built into the almost entirely ethereal social bondage within the 'networked' societies of today. As compared to humans just over half a century ago, individual members of the species today are far more taciturn and incapable of relating to other members of the species. The urbanised and networked habitats created by the preceding generations are currently the sites of silence within which the ease of human-to-human communication is no longer possible without the mediation of a vast range of man-made memory and speech devices.

It is as if we are being enveloped on all sides by a sea of silence in which we cannot stay afloat despite all our massive communication gadgetry. Alienation, which marked the initial phase of modernity, has now attained a higher pitch and scale, escape from which requires constant and repeated reminders of the self in the form of 'selfies'.

After spending nearly half a million years in forming human societies, we seem to have struck the mood of a 'specific' reversal brought about by an unprecedented isolation of members of the species. We have perhaps arrived at a juncture where being social is possible only in the dimensionless reality of cyberspace, within which signifiers seem to have been stripped of their conventionally associated signification.

6

Then there is yet another more chilling, and at the same time, more exciting experience of silence into which we are moving as rapidly as a water-strider—a bug—caught in a giant waterfall. It appears that human communication is getting ready to go beyond, or outside, the verbal language that we have used over the last 70,000 years.

Natural languages based on verbal icons are dwindling in our time as if a mysterious epidemic has struck them at the root.

Whether this is due to neurological changes affecting the human brain, or an expression of the evolutionary processes guiding us through time, or the inauguration of a new era of knowledge-gathering by the human consciousness, the experience of it all now, in our generation, is profoundly unsettling.

7

This three-faced silence, arising out of power dynamics, technology-driven social changes and neurological-evolutionary compulsions, has brought back to us the responsibility of reflecting on the nature of silence, our collective negotiation with it, the consequences it entails for the human consciousness—both, *what* it knows and *how* it knows—and the very idea of being human.

It is therefore that I thought of reflecting on the question of silence. I should add that reflecting on silence through words and sentences is a contradiction in terms. Yet, there is no known method of 'writing' without words. Such a method shall no doubt be known to humans and followed widely at some future date. In fact, the pervasive silences surrounding us all point to that imminent possibility. However, at this early stage of the new phase in human existence—which is one of the themes in this volume—I have chosen a form that is significantly different from the conventional forms of written books. The apparently unrelated shorter sections in it are all records of a memory-scape, without any fiction. I shall not be surprised if this manner of presenting my argument is dismissed as unacceptable by some readers. However, my hope is that even if the content of my argument does not achieve what it seeks to, perhaps its unconventional composition may help in pointing to what I wish to explore—namely, the question of silence.

8

Initially, when I was planning this book, I had thought I would use a number of my interviews on the theme of dying languages in order to bring home the language situation at present. Most of them were occasioned by the announcement of the People's Linguistic Survey of India (PLSI). Since the context of the PLSI was perceived to be the sudden and pervasive decline in natural languages—while my own interest in the work was founded on the desire to celebrate diversity—the questioners invariably prodded me to break the bad news of the death of this or that language. This was my experience in talking to correspondents from major Indian newspapers and journals, as well as those from the US, Germany, France and Japan.

After the slew of interviews came to pass, and I found some quiet time and space for assessing the impact of the PLSI, I felt it necessary to address the questions in the minds of those who did not have an opportunity to ask them through personal conversations. Sifting through those interviews, I thought it would help if I were to select a few and put them together with the purpose of addressing those questions. This I wanted to do not out of vanity—of which I am amply guilty—but out of a need to capture and perhaps preserve the fleeting glimpses of something larger that I had come close to witnessing during the PLSI work, beyond the mere rise and fall of languages as in past eras of human ascent. These glimpses led me to imagining a future for humans that would have a language of a very different kind, produced, pitched and perceived very differently, and within an altogether different genre of performance. I shall try to articulate in a future work what that future language can be. For the present work, I have only attempted to tentatively point in that direction through this para-biography intended as a metaphor.

9

When the PLSI was in progress, the frequency with which I was asked to speak to large gatherings of scholars increased well beyond what it had been during my earlier years as a literary scholar and, later, as a cultural activist. Since I had made a somewhat uncommon migration from the field of literary criticism to anthropology, and from there to linguistics, and since I have engaged with academic as well as activist fields in my life, I was required to give lectures to a rather wide range of interest groups. To save myself from the risk of becoming entirely superficial, I developed the habit of speaking to very small groups of friends on themes of my choice. This protected my space for experimenting with thought and presenting what a larger public gathering would rarely have appreciated or found of interest. In these conversations, I attempted to draw my audience's attention to the less visible processes of change affecting our collective destinies. These processes, taken together, could be termed natural evolution, though one is aware that trillions of micro-changes are actively involved in that larger process which the normal human intellect can comprehend but fleetingly.

What was articulated in those involved conversations was based on my thinking and cognition. Therefore, I felt it was necessary to track down the roots of those ideas in terms of what I had actually seen, experienced, stored and restored in my mind. In attempting such a task, the normal convention of discursive writing would have led me to writing my 'intellectual autobiography'. However, I do not believe that the ideas that have come up in my previous works even remotely place me anywhere close to that lofty rank of thinkers. What this text presents is merely a para-biography, and not a history of ideas as they evolved in my work. My interest in writing it was to observe, in earnest, how, as a member of this vast (and sadly, supremely arrogant) species, my mind and thought were being impacted by the many silences around me—political, social and verbal.

10

Silence, '*shanti*', has been an abiding interest for visionaries and thinkers in all civilisations. Various traditions of aesthetics have devoted significant thought to unraveling the mystery and beauty that silence holds within it. The *tantra* tradition of poetics articulated by Abhinavagupta makes '*shant*' the *summum bonum* of aesthetic relish. Theologists have spoken about the 'silence' at the beginning of Creation; mystics, Sufis and saint-poets have sung paeans to silence.

However, the silence one is thinking of in our time has a different and terrifying quality, with its roots in the Nazi concentration camps and State-sponsored genocides. It brings to mind the images of those who perished without a word facing nuclear arms assaults like those in Hiroshima, Nagasaki, gas leakages like in Bhopal, or in radiation disasters like Chernobyl. The idea of silence evokes those millions of faces of starving children in Somalia and thousands on the run out of Syria, ready for a death by drowning. The women in India's north-eastern states facing rapes by the custodians of law and honour, the tribals in central India falling to bullets in the name of either a revolution or the law, followers of diverse faiths burnt and killed in many parts of the world—all of these are the visible, perceivable images of silence in our time. These are at least visible. Then there are also the countless invisible speech communities that have lost their native tongues, only occasionally reported in the *National Geographic* or similar media. All of us, almost without exception—the severely alienated, isolated, unable to experience relations in any depth—too, are marooned in silence in our time. In a way, the question of silence is as important for us, or perhaps even more important, than the question of violence in our time. The following pages are an attempt to understand and articulate various contours and shades of that question as experienced by me during the unchartered course of my inner life.

11

This work is not academic. It is not a literary work. It does not belong to a set genre as fiction or non-fiction. It is not *about* silence. It is about my engagement with silence. There is a lot more I could have written in it, but the heart no longer desires to speak. And so I bring this work to you reluctantly, without any 'authorial will' compelling me to.

If I were to willingly write a book on disappearing languages and the shrinking space for expression, I would have presented the entire journey of my exploration of the hundreds of Indian languages resulting in the People's Linguistic Survey of India. The project has been monumental in scale and epic in the vastness of exploration. The challenges faced along the way and the learnings gleaned from the struggle certainly deserve to be written as a book-length account of that intellectual adventure. Despite having spent the past decade working 17 hours a day, 365 days a year on the PLSI, I do not find the journey exhilarating. Rather, it is the purely clinical face of silence that I have encountered amidst all the dying languages that has left me dazed. For me the silence enveloping our languages is no longer abstract like an experience but very real like a locust, a thing and not just an impression. Its vision pains me at heart. Having seen it, I now speak with difficulty, write without the desire to write, spell words without recall of memory and end up producing wrongly spelt words somehow strung together into ungainly sentences. Instead of writing a theoretical treatise, I have chosen to bring together my words, which have by now started becoming strangers to me.

12

In the past I have spent long spells trying to understand silence, that which results from the pursuit of some profound enigma, as well as that which results from the breakdown of dialogue or suppression of voice.

As a young man, having gone through my quota of cynicism, Marxism, modernity and recklessness, I came close to mysticism—much of which I have lost long ago—and launched upon a study of the sage of Pondicherry. My 20-something mind was trying to understand how a firebrand revolutionary could plunge into the mysteries of the Vedas and turn to a lifelong silence, spending a stretch of 24 years—1926 to 1950—in a single room, presenting himself to the world for a *darshana* just four days a year. I read his poems written during these years to see if his words could bring forth the faintest glimmer of the silence that he experienced. It was like going on an interminable outer-space voyage where one could forget the grammar of one's own speech. Sri Aurobindo's was a language of colours, not words, and the colours were not those that the human eye can see. The idea of this all-enveloping silence as the high-street in a cosmic journey—of which the human journey along the path of evolution is but a fragment—has remained in my mind as an elusive memory of the future.

My move from rural Kolhapur in Maharashtra to the mercilessly beautiful city of Baroda was prompted by a desire to work in the university where, nine decades before my time, Sri Aurobindo had taught. But, he slipped out of my mind soon after I arrived in Baroda as I started making frequent visits to the tribal villages in eastern Gujarat. These villages were filled with a different kind of silence. A silence which was tangible as it could be known as an experience by my very irrational mind. Besides, it spoke of a history that made one sad and angry at the same time. I then thought that creating a space for the voice of the Adivasis would be one way of breaking this other silence. And so for much of my time of three and a half decades in Baroda, I became an active advocate of that voice, a voice-activist.

Yet, despite my activism, the lure of the cosmic silence kept surfacing in my mind from time to time. And when it became too seductive to ignore, I shared my thoughts through lectures given to small groups of friends. These lectures were partly a cure for my weakening resolve, and partly an invitation for me to explore new frontiers of thought. The lectures were not based on written texts. From my school days, I have developed a dislike for cold lectures. I like them only if they are made in the moment of articulation like a good hot *roti* being baked on the *chulha* fire.

On a few occasions, persons who happened to be in Baroda to visit me asked me if they could record what I was saying. Since I did not care either way, I consented. Later, these recordings were transcribed by one enthusiastic friend. I have included a few short excerpts of that transcription in this book as a record of my inner struggles, of being torn between human voices and the future cosmic silence. The transition from the one to the other will be necessarily violent, alas. The sites of that imminent violence cannot be left unattended as *fate accompli*.

13

My life in Baroda as a university teacher was marked with a generous quota of conferences and fellowships. In order to be able to do what is normally not done, I did all of those things that are normally to be done, quite meticulously, so that I would not stand out as one beyond the pale of norms. During the mid-nineties, working on a fellowship, I devoted myself to the study of violence, conversing with under-trial prisoners and analysing past philosophers who had reflected on violence. As I kept visiting those individuals in their jail cells, discussing the murders they had committed, one thing that became clear to me was that conversations have a habit of breaking down. When the breakdown becomes too severe, dialogue becomes impossible and an undesirable silence dominates, relations become impossible and thought acquires the colours of violence.

My venerable old friend Gandhi—and I adore him—was known for placing in circulation a pair of words: truth and non-violence. I could understand what violence was, but I had considerable difficulty with truth. It was not easy for me to decide on the objective conditions of truth, for one man's truth can be another's untruth. It was during my conversation with the jail mates that one day I chanced upon a more manageable meaning of the term. I thought 'one's work to create a society free of violence' is truth. So, non-violence is the goal, truth the path to it. One must contribute one's bit in paving that path; howsoever insignificant, yet one must.

I do not like to imitate and I detest becoming enslaved by ideas, even when they are charming and promise liberty, salvation or power. Gandhi is good, I thought, but not for me to imitate. I adore Charlie Chaplin, but do not dress like him. So, I resolved for myself that my search for truth lies in reducing the potential for violence and in trying to foster dialogue. This took me to the tribals, to unraveling their silence, fighting their aphasia. Tribals, as land-holding Adivasis as well as the dispossessed nomadic communities that had undeservingly become the victims of a stigma, captured all my attention.

14

British colonial rule in India was not only a political and economic enterprise; it was also an experiment in restructuring a complex society. For the first two centuries of colonial contact, beginning with the arrival of the East India Company at Surat in 1600 to the establishment of the Asiatic Society in Bengal towards the end of the eighteenth century, the colonial imagination had great difficulties in understanding the complex weaves of Indian society. Out of these difficulties arose many misconceptions and myths about communities and social conventions. At times these were as comical and absurd as the idea that India is a country of snake charmers and magicians. But in many instances their wrong reading of our society resulted in untold human misery. This very same 'knowledge' formed the basis for formulating laws during colonial times. The history of the communities known as 'denotified' is without doubt one of the most mind-boggling sagas of the collapse of compassion, reason and humanity.

During the 1830s, the colonial government appointed William Henry Sleeman (1788–1856) to prepare a list of instances of assaults on wayfarers in central India. Sleeman took to this task with amazing devotion and produced a voluminous list of violent episodes. This list would not have amounted to much had it not been for the turn of events during 1857 in central India. In the wake of the battles fought and lost by the Indian states, all isolated and potential groups of soldiers, and even those who were likely to be in the supply chain for them, came to be seen as candidates for the Sleeman-list. Later, it was this list that became the basis of the 1871 Criminal Tribes Act (CTA).

15

Once the traditional occupations of the nomadic and semi-nomadic communities were brought under the scanner, the colonial government provided for their being officially declared 'Criminal Tribes'. The government's powers to declare a community 'criminal' were made arbitrary to the extent that the question of inclusion of a given community in the list was taken completely out of the judiciary's purview. After this, even an attempt by any member of the community to move out of the district without informing the local authorities became a punishable offence. The act of questioning the notification in any form, too, came to be seen as a criminal offence.

The colonial government's right to detain such communities and to do whatever the government decided to do with their lives came to be seen as a lawful right and duty of the government officials. The officials were charged to prepare 'Registers of Criminal Tribes', and once a register was prepared for a given district, even the official who prepared it was not allowed to make any deletions in it. The nature of the declaration was made entirely non-negotiable and absolute.

The victims of this draconian law were given no legal reprieve. The onus of proving that they were not criminal fell on them, but they were left with no rational argument since their being born in a certain community itself was seen as a crime. Individuals belonging to these tribes had to spend their entire lives proving to the authorities without any specific reason that they were not criminals. Thus, life itself became a trial for them without any let up whatsoever.

The communities 'notified' under the 1871 Act acquired the form of some 'social raw material' for use in empire-building. Members of these communities came to be used in the colonial construction projects of railways, roads and factories. The law legitimised the right of the administrators to bundle up and shunt them about as and when and wherever they were perceived to be of use: 'Any tribes, gang or class, which has been declared to be criminal, or any part thereof, may, by order of the local government, be removed to any other place of residence.'[1] Even the children of these communities were not viewed with any special sympathy. The government decided that the superintendent of the specific settlement was to be asked to function as the 'mother' for such children.

The infamous CTA dictated forced 'isolation' and 'reform' of the communities listed thereunder. These included coin-makers, entertainers, migratory peasants, stray wandering groups, nomadic communities, long-distance traders and such others. The CTA required the creation of 'settlements' as reformatories with 'strict procedures'. These procedures kept becoming increasingly inhuman. Forced labour became the daily fate of the inmates. The CTA of 1871 went through several revisions, every revision bringing in new forms of 'punishment' for being born within the listed communities. The last of the CTA was passed in 1924. By then a total of 191 communities had been brought under its purview.

16

About the same time as the CTA was getting formulated, the colonial government produced another list of communities under the caption 'the Tribes of India'. These were the communities that had come in conflict with the British rule on the issue of imposition of the government's sovereign authority over the forest areas. During the 1860s, the British had created a forest department, primarily to provide good quality timber for building railways and naval ships. The forest-dwelling communities of India opposed the colonial takeover of their forests and habitats. They neither cared for the colonial government nor did they understand the idiom of British law. Not surprisingly, most of these conflicts were violent and involved armed clashes. Since the political and everyday idioms of the conflicting parties were radically divergent, it became difficult for the colonial government and its diplomacy to forge treaties with the forest-dwelling communities.

Communities located at all such areas of conflict were bundled together by the colonial government under the term 'tribe'. Soon after, as the need to conceptualise and classify 'tribes' became clearer, a sophisticated machinery of scholarship was put in place to enumerate, describe and define the numerous Indian tribes. The historical, linguistic and cultural differences among these communities were so vast and complex that it would have been impossible for any rational scheme of sociological classification to place them in a single conceptual category.

While all this was happening in India's political history, already a branch of Orientalism had emerged in Europe in the form of anthropology, perhaps more appropriately termed 'savageology'. Some of the attributes discussed in 'savageology' were applied to Indian 'tribes', which then came to be seen as necessarily primitive.

By the end of the nineteenth century, the concept of tribe and the notion of criminal tribes had received acceptance even among educated Indians—writers, journalists and lawyers. As a result, when the 1891 version of the CTA was enacted, or when the register of forest codes was prepared the following year, there was no evident protest from any quarter. By the turn of the century, 'tribe' had come to stay as an unchallenged category constitutive of *the primitive* in Indian society.

17

When, during the 1980s, I started noticing the alarming disparity between the development of other classes and communities on the one hand, and the development of the Adivasis and Denotified Tribes (DNTs) on the other, I felt drawn to exploring the link between denial of access to the means of development and the 'structural aphasia' imposed on the marginalised languages. Towards this end, 'Bhasha', which means language or voice, was founded in 1996 as a Research and Publication Centre for the documentation and study of literature in Adivasi languages. The ultimate horizon of obligations for Bhasha at the moment of its inception was to document and publish fifty bilingual volumes of Adivasi literature. Little did I know as its founder that beyond the horizon, many new worlds were waiting for it!

Within months of commencing work on the 50-volume series, many Adivasi writers and scholars approached me with the idea of starting a magazine in their own languages aimed at the Adivasi communities, and to be read out rather than for individual reading. Bhasha accepted the idea. The magazine was called *Dhol* (or drums), a term that has a totemic cultural significance for the Adivasis. We started using the state scripts combined with a moderate use of diacritics to represent these languages. The response to the magazine was tremendous. More Adivasis approached Bhasha and asked for versions of *Dhol* in their own languages. In two years' time *Dhol* started appearing in ten Adivasi languages: Kunkna, Ahirani, God Banjara, Bhantu, Dehwali, Pawari, Rathwi, Chaudhari, Panchamahali Bhilli, and Dungra Bhilli, respectively. When the first issue of *Dhol* in Chaudhari language was released at the Padam-Dungri village in South Gujarat, it sold 700 copies in less than an hour. This was a record of sorts for a little magazine.

Inspired by the success of the oral magazine, our Adivasi collaborators started bringing manuscripts of their autobiographies, poems, essays and anthropological studies of their communities which they wanted us to publish. Subsequently, in order to highlight the oral nature of Adivasi culture, we launched a weekly radio magazine which was relayed throughout the Adivasi areas of Gujarat and Maharashtra. All these initiatives together gave birth to a small but focused publishing and book distribution house, which now works under the name 'Purva-Prakash' and is the first community-owned publishing programme for Adivasis and DNTs. Purva-Prakash has been a self-supporting though not so much a commercial venture as a cultural and literary platform for intellectual concerns, and a forum for expression in the people's own languages.

Oral literature, unlike written literature, is not an exclusive verbal or lexical art. It is inevitably intermixed with song, music, dance, ritual and craft. So, Bhasha was drawn to the craft of Adivasi communities, initially in western India, and subsequently from all over India. This resulted in Bhasha's craft collection and craft training initiatives, further leading to the formation of an Adivasi craft cooperative under the name 'Tribals First'. The objects one identifies as craft are not produced in Adivasi communities for aesthetic pleasure alone. They are an integral part of their daily life. Often such objects carry with them an imprint of the supernatural as conceived in their myth and imagination. The shapes, colours and forms of these objects reflect the transactions in the Adivasi collective unconscious. Often one overlooks the fact that the metaphysical matrix of the Adivasi thought process differs markedly from the philosophic assumptions of the dominant cultural traditions in India. Therefore, sometimes simple concepts and ideas, which look perfectly natural and secular, can provoke Adivasis into reacting negatively, and even violently.

18

My journey into the minds and lives of Adivasis and the nomads has been long. It was not easy, though never tiresome, for that was my path to truth. Along this journey, I met countless great personalities, each one illuminating my life in a different way. But one of them made her mark the most. With her, I worked, travelled, sang old movie songs, but most of all discussed for hours and hours how she understood the everlasting silence, the one that Shakespeare had in mind when he said, 'The rest is silence'. She, too, was a writer of the order to which Shakespeare belongs.

She was difficult and indomitable. Invariably, she would say, 'I do not know. All that I know is I would like to find my eternal rest under a tree at the Adivasi Academy'. In August 2016, a week after she passed away in Kolkata, Surekha and I brought her mortal remains to Tejgad and placed them in an earthen urn at the place she had chosen for herself. She now complements my work of encouraging the voices of the oppressed by adding her silence to it.

Though all of my time over the last three decades has been spent in espousing a republic of threatened voices, and though the linguistic survey I undertook has been seen by some as an amazing experiment of giving these suppressed and unheard voices their due legitimacy, I have chosen in this book not to write about my work with the nomads and tribals, and about what an epic struggle it was to bring the PLSI into this world. This book is not about me. It is about the silence that is beginning to surround us on all sides. This book may best be read as an activist act—the act of pointing to the phenomena that make being human a challenge, once again.

19

There are several known speech disorders. Going by the names used in medical science, it appears that they were identified in the West in ancient times when the Greek language ruled supreme. Amnesia, hysteria, euphoria and dyslexia are some of the more prominent among them. Autism is a modern addition to these terms. None of these affect the body as other diseases do. But, as the word is the only means by which humans can come to terms with the world, any speech aberration can easily affect one's relation with the world. Recent research shows that dyslectic children are more gifted in cognitive abilities than linguistically normal children. Neuroscience believes that the increasing unease with written language that children have started showing is an early symptom of an evolutionary shift. Similarly, autism is often a result of a higher sensitivity towards touch and sound. It enables autistic children to perceive the world very differently than linguistically normal children. Dyslexia and autism are not easily reversible. Amnesia leads to the mind's ordering of memory in many innovative ways. An amnesiac's memory is in many ways a rich source of creativity.

The most dreaded among speech-related diseases is aphasia. It means simply the loss of speech. Since speech distinguishes humans from other animals, aphasia becomes for its victim the very negation of being human. It should not be equated with muteness, which is no more than a purely physical disorder. The mute, as also the hearing-impaired, can construct highly complex language by using signs. Such sign languages exist in all parts of the world. They have their unique grammar, sentence patterns and vocabulary.

Aphasia, unlike the mere physical inability to speak, is a neurological disorder. In it, the brain fails to generate language signals or it fails to guide the vocal chords to receive the signals and enact them. Aphasia is manifestation of the discord between the brain and the body. This comes about due to a serious aberration in the part of the brain that regulates not only language transactions but also those parts that regulate abstraction and judgement. Doctors have to carry out extremely complicated brain-imaging, corrective therapy and tongue training before a patient of aphasia can be even partially cured.

I have often used the term 'aphasia' in my work related with tribal languages. The coercive State and the continuously sliding human development index of the Adivasis have turned them reticent. We rarely hear them speak up against the many forms of injustice they have to face as their daily lot. When they speak at all, their expression is perceived by society as a rejection of the State. I worked for nearly two decades with various Adivasi groups for creating spaces for their expression. Of course, I was not dealing with neurological aphasia but a sociological one. In the process, I learnt a lot about how this social aphasia sets in and how it can be cured.

Recently, when the four senior judges of the apex Indian court spoke up, the term aphasia came back in my thoughts. The disconnect between the Chief Justice and the senior judges can be diagnosed in terms of the neurology and linguistics of aphasia. If the analogy is pressed further, the episode can be read as an indication of not only the state of the judiciary but also that of the legislative wing and the executive wing of the Indian State. The rot is much deeper. Citizens have been witnessing it in the form of an unprecedented circulation of abusive language in public discourse, hysterical TV debates, arrogant browbeating of hapless citizens by their own chosen leaders and unimaginative and autistic commentators. The official interpretations of the judges' statement as 'a manufactured dissent' and 'conspiracy' are the ultimate indicator of a serious discord between the brain and the body of Indian polity. In order to cure it, we all need to question the aphasia being imposed on us.

20

The nature of the State has fundamentally changed over the last three decades throughout the world. Certain characteristics that were exhibited by autocratic regimes in the past have now entered the self-understanding of the State in democracies as well.

Previously such autocratic regimes were described by the global community of nations as 'rogue nations'. The 'rogue nations' were the ones who showed no respect for established norms of decency in relation with their own people as well as in relation with other nations. In the second decade of the twentieth century, though democracies have not plummeted to those depths, they have slowly started becoming indifferent to some of the basic democratic values in relation to their own people. This is so particularly in respect of the ethnic, linguistic or religious sections that do not count much in electoral terms. The term commonly used for such insensitivity to the marginal social groups is 'majoritarian rule'. The phenomenon is widespread from Turkey, Egypt, Russia, China and the US to Ukraine, Austria, Spain and our own country. The spread of the new slant in democracies cannot be brushed aside by thinking of it in terms of certain personality cults or as historical accidents. It calls for a reasoned explanation.

Three important developments over the last three decades appear to be at the heart of the matter. The most visible of these is the rise of corporate power and its debilitating impact on the State's ability to make decisions. The relatively less visible but equally important is the near collapse of international organisations and the waning of their ability to regulate nations and maintain a balance of power among them. The third reason is the enormous increase in the role of technology in every aspect of life in its individual and collective forms.

These three together form a single narrative. Stated in plain words, it says that an increased engagement with technology is synonymous with progress. In order to enhance the control of technology, an increasingly free play be made possible for the ever-spreading corporate. And finally, for providing the space for the corporate, the State carves out large chunks of its own authority as well as obligations. The cumulative result of this narrative is the need to silence people, particularly those who are marginal and those who question this new understanding of the State's responsibility towards the people who constitute it.

In this new order of democracies, we have started witnessing repression of the people with an unprecedented frequency. It is not that there has been no precedence whether in France or in Italy or in China or in India. General de Gaulle had dealt with the young generation of his time with the same ruthless might as the successive Italian governments had with the Communists. There has been no shortage of instances in India when perfectly peaceful agitators have been dealt by the State with uncalled for violence. But, in those instances, the nations, political parties, people and media thought it fit to condemn the unfair use of violence. Over the last three decades, the voices that condemn the State's use of violence against its hapless people have gradually become silent, or have been silenced. What is worse is that the word remorse is no longer in circulation in the political lexicon. The perpetrators have learnt to justify the denial of democratic spaces through flat denials.

In recent times, the killings of innocent individuals by vigilantes, killings of intellectuals by zealots, cold-blooded hacking of political opponents, insults hurled at Adivasis, Dalits, women and minorities have all shown in their aftermath that the feeling of remorse is banished from our public discourse. The silence of the government on denial of democratic space for any dissention is now the norm. This silence needs to be questioned if democracies have to be kept in life.

21

Ever since the rise of the 'egoistic sublime' during the Romantic Revolution in the early nineteenth century in Germany and England, writing self-life narratives has become a temptation for many, in poetry, in fiction and in plain prose. At the same time, ever since the industrial civilisation started giving rise to densely populated urban habitats, the voyeurism of readers has provided the necessary sociology for the expression of the self. In our time, the selfie is, ironically, fast becoming the supreme ritual of socialisation. I do not think I can write an autobiography. Not everything in life can be said. The last part of this book is not in any sense a linear story of my life. It is not even a selective autobiography. It is an attempt at capturing how I see silence and voice. It is a statement of why I see aphasia where others see noise, and why I see silence where others see the euphoria of progress. It is an attempt at seeing how I see. I have done it by recalling my encounters with different cities at different times in my life. It should not be mistaken in any way as my intellectual autobiography. Most of the ideas that have fascinated me have been perennial ideas that have had life before my time. I just happened to have a brush with them. I am content in staking a claim to my utter lack of originality.

Had I been Cox Habbema, or had she been me in 2017, there would have been an investigation of the three narratives of silence. That becomes for me, and for us, the question of silence. I have tried to state it through a hackneyed, non-linear, self-tormenting testimony, through a metaphor for our enigmas rather than through a forensic narrative of our time.

Notes

[1] *Criminal Tribes Act*, 1871, cited in G. N. Devy, 'Introduction', in *The Oxford India Elwin*, Verrier Elwin and G. N. Devy (New Delhi: Oxford University Press, 2008).

2 Silence on the Horizon[*]

1

It has been a convention to depict on the cover page of the *Bhagwad-Gita* the image of Arjuna on a chariot with Sri Krishna as the charioteer. The convention is so well established that the printed *Gita* may appear almost incomplete without this visual preface. Krishna as seen in this image has one arm twined with the reigns of the horses, storming into the war-field. The other arm of Krishna is shown as slightly raised towards the skies, with one of his fingers supporting the *sudarshan chakra*. The *chakra* of Krishna is described in ancient Indian mythology as Krishna's weapon, the ultimate weapon with unmatched divine power and which has been gifted to Krishna alone.

It is not quite clear if the *Bhagwad-Gita* was a part of the *Mahabharata* from the earliest phase of the Mahabharata lore,

---

* Author's note: A part of this essay was previously published in my essay 'Changing Script', in Rita Kothari ed. *Multilingual Nation: Translation and Language Dynamic in India* (New Delhi: Oxford University Press, 2018), and is reproduced here with the kind permission of Rita Kothari, and Oxford University Press.

when it was known as *Jaya-Itihasa,* or whether it was added to the ever-growing epic in some later period. What is clear, though, is that the chakra—the wheel—has been at the heart of the *Mahabharata* story. This one is called the *kala-chakra,* indicating the inexorable flow of events in human time, or *kala*. There is no doubt that in its earliest form, and in the numerous regional versions across the country in which the *Mahabharata* emerged and continued to exist throughout history, the plot of the epic is centred around an epoch-making war. The philosophical burden that the work is made to carry is probably the result of many additions to the narrative in the form of long discussions and expositions; and it is not unlikely that the idea of a *kala-purusha* as the primary narrator and the depiction of the kala-chakra as the central thread of the epic are the results of some such additions. Whatever may be the case, the wheel motif has come to be seen as being of the very essence of this ancient Indian epic.

The wheel motif appears once again in a powerful and evocative visual form in the ancient sculpture at Sarnath. The *dhamma-chakra* brings the chakra of the kala-purusha to meet the philosophical reflections of the Buddha. It is interesting to note that the concept of chakra pre-dates both the *Mahabharata* and the Buddha. The term 'chakra' has been traced to the language or languages considered to have been the ancestors of both Sanskrit and Pali. It is also present in several other languages that are believed to have arisen out of the proto-Indo-European language—ancestor to many of the major languages of what is today described as the 'ancient world', including Latin, Greek, Sanskrit, Turkish among several others. Historical linguistics tells us that 'there was probably a word "*kwekwlos*", meaning "wheel", which is the ancestor of "*kuklos*" in classical Greek, of "kakra" in Old Indic and—because "k" shifts to "h" in Germanic languages—of "*hweohl*" in Old English, itself the ancestor of "wheel" in modern English.'[1] Thus, 'wheel' or 'chakra' has been of use in thought for those who spoke the earliest forms of Greek, Indic and Germanic languages, and is a concept older than these languages and inherited from an earlier time, an earlier culture and an earlier language.

It would, of course, be simplistic to imagine that this 'earlier' language or culture was a homogenous one and spread over a vast part of the earth. It would be more appropriate in this respect to imagine that the idea of the chakra was of use to many cultures and languages in the period prior to the times we now know as 'ancient times'. Indeed, it was so ever since the rise of agriculture as a dominant mode of production started playing a key role in economies in different parts of what is now known as Europe and Asia. Various researches in archaeology, linguistics, genetics and related sciences indicate that this period prior to the known ancient times extends between 9,000 years to 6,500 years before our times. Those two or three millennia witnessed the rise of agriculture as a mode of production, and the rise of the concept of the wheel. Researches in archaeology and linguistics indicate that it was during these very millennia that humans started developing communication systems based on verbal signs.

As to the question whether human societies had any comparable communication systems prior to this prolonged phase, the answer so far accepted as the most dependable is that while there were 'languages' prior to the shift from hunting-gathering economies to pastoral-agrarian economies, practically all of them diminished and were replaced by the 'pre-ancient' languages. These pre-ancient languages were—as symbolic systems of meaning—not too dissimilar from the languages in use in our time, and significantly different from the languages that existed before them. Since agriculture was the moving force in their emergence, let us refer to them—purely metaphorically—as the *chakra* languages.

2

We have said that the languages of the chakra millennia were, as systems of meaning, fairly close to those in use in our time. But we need to enter one caveat here—none of them were ever 'represented' in the form of writing. On the other hand, in our time we have firmly accepted the idea that a mature language is one which has a well-defined system of representation in writing and is therefore capable of being printed for long-distance distribution. Writing brings natural languages to a new phase of communication. In this form, and particularly when writing is aided by printing technologies, what is spoken can be carried from one epoch to another and from one geographical location to another geographical location with a great degree of accuracy. Of course, meanings of words shift from location to location and more decidedly, from epoch to epoch; but that slide or shift is a limitation—one may even say, a gift—that natural languages have to carry with them as a kind of a birthmark. The very nature of 'meaning' itself makes it impossible to reproduce or replicate. However, if we set aside this more philosophical difficulty, it becomes clear that writing, with all its myriad variations, places natural languages within a historical phase that is significantly different from the chakra phase. Using, once again, a metaphor, let us call this written phase of language the *scale* phase, for the emergence of writing is very closely associated with the rise of economic transactions that associated 'value' to production, initially agricultural production.

Scripts were initially conceptualised to record complex economic transactions involving production, which was seen as not just materials but as materials with economic value. It included human labour. It also included inheritance or property. Thus, in ancient times natural languages started asking to be scripted when the speech communities using them developed production practices, giving rise to the concept of 'surplus', 'exchange' and 'value'—all economic values. In ancient Indian mythology, in *Puranic* lore as well as in the Buddhist *Jatakas*, the mention of the merchant class is common. The earliest holders of letters were traders, although subsequently the writing classes assumed the functions of administrators, legislators and priests. The economic history of societies in various parts of the world, together with the history of languages that were strengthened by writing as a means of representing speech, has profoundly affected the fate of the natural languages inherited by humans from pre-ancient times.

3

The number of natural languages that have come down to our time is phenomenally large. It is believed that there are at least about 6,000 living languages today. Not all of them originate in one and the same historical period. Some are but a century old while others have a history running over millennia. While some of these languages can be described using a linguistic description that we recognise as grammar, not all of them have grammars that fit into a single descriptive framework. There are several languages that show exceptional behaviour, and if all these exceptions are put together, they render a shared grammatical description meaningless. What is, however, common to all these languages—except the sign languages—is that all of them use voice or sound to signify meaning. It is true that writing—which is not speech but only a representation of speech or rather an illusion of sound—removes language from its verbal basis. Yet, without the verbal basis the representation cannot acquire sense. At least, this was so until fairly recent times.

Language is normally understood as words and sentences. A collection of verbal icons put together rather arbitrarily and settled in their meaning by convention. A vast game played collectively whose rules are never clearly spelt out but tacitly understood and accepted by the speakers. However, language is not merely the business of speaking and sound. Language originates in silence and ends in silence. And as a constant reminder of this perpetually forgotten truth we punctuate every spoken sentence with silent gaps between words. Without those gaps, those pauses—what the Latin poetics called *caesurae*—words would cease to carry meaning.

The silent pauses in a sentence are not an aesthetic embellishment but an absolute and non-negotiable requirement for the realisation of meaning. This is so because the human brain, unlike the brains of other animal species, is recursive. In other words, the human brain not only thinks, as brains in other species do, but it also thinks *about* thinking. This being so, when one speaks one not only formulates words to be uttered but also thinks of the thought or cognition it causes in the listener's brain. We do so while speaking as well as while writing. Pauses between words are introduced primarily for the benefit of the cognitive activity of the listening or the reading brain. The non-verbal, non-linguistic pauses are the silence that operates as the framework for meaning to become possible. It is this silence knitted together with verbal icons that enables language to be an effective vehicle of meaning and helps us set it apart from noise.

The substance of silence contained within the pauses between words is significantly different from any endless silence in an imaginary vacuum in space. The silence of an imagined vacuum could be utter absence of meaning and movement. The silences woven into speech are, in contrast, dynamic and potent: the *sachetana* not the *achetana*.

In the process of evolution, the recursive quality of the human brain was first recognised through the exchange of visual signals with the help of the eye rather than the ear.

Like communication in the case of most other animal species, human communication, too, began through visual exchanges. Approximately half a million years ago, it became associated with body movements, the shaking of the head, the waving of hands, the bending of the body and the movement of arms and legs. That phase of communication seems to have lasted for over 200,000 years. During this prolonged phase, humans learned to associate thought in the brain with body movement. Gradually, greater complexities in body movements led to the movement of facial muscles, involving the lips, teeth, tongue and nose. This in turn helped humans to discover that clicking of the tongue and stretching of the lips could help regulate the air-flow to produce a certain predictable quality of pitch and tone. Yet, the learning was slow. It took humans another 200,000 years or more to arrive at a well-regulated tonal language. Language as we know it today is barely 70,000 years old. And that is not too long a period in the entire process of human evolution.

Given that communication has not been bound to verbal icons alone in the ages past, it is not improbable that the *Homo sapiens* species moves on from verbal communication to another medium of communication. Of course, for this to happen there must be some significant gain that the brain sees in the use of another medium. But sad will be the day when that transformation takes place, for it will spell the death of all beauty, complexity and the magic that language in verbal icons has been. Yet, whether we like it or not, such a transformation has already started taking place. The physical aspects of speech are already being challenged and altogether transformed.

Various modes of linguistic representation have impacted 'language as speech' to such an extent that possibilities of languages that are almost entirely dissociated from speech have started beckoning the human mind. The digital world provides one such possibility. The digitised exchange of meaning, communication without sound, can be compared to a shadow play where shadows signify substance in absence of what the shadows stand for within the visual field of the onlooker.

The idea that shadow has a remarkable referential capacity and versatile signification ability is not a recent idea. It occurs in ancient Greek philosophy as it does in the *Upanishads*. In our time, as the 6,000 living languages are caught in a survival crisis, there is an amazing growth in the universe of 'shadow meaning', in the exchange of human thought and memory, through the phenomenally speedy exchange of digits. Perhaps, it is an indication of the emergence of an altogether new form of communication.

4

Being enveloped in language for the past several millennia, humans have learnt to conceptualise Time and Space as the definitive categories and (pre)conditions of being. The ability of the human brain to make images enables it to make sense of the space surrounding us. Human memory allows us to weave together an idea of time, and then to negotiate it. Both these 'faculties'—first given to us by the ability to transact meaning through symbolic icons and then transformed into a myriad externalised forms—have come to be seen as having always existed as an apparatus that helps construct the peculiarly human 'worldview'. The externalised forms of imagination have guided both our aesthetics and our collective life. The externalised forms of memory have come to form the very foundations of what we see today as 'knowledge'—in objective and institutionalised forms.

This progression in the course of man's cognitive and cultural evolution has led to a collective amnesia of the process of natural evolution, of which the human animal, too, is a creature. Time as we understand it, human time, is not a natural phenomenon. It is but a convenient figment of human imagination. Ditto perhaps for space; for, space that the human eye sees and space that the visual faculty of millions of other species apprehends are in all probability so radically divergent that any 'objective' measure of space becomes a joke. If one takes such a stark view of the human perception of space and time, it follows that human imagination that constructs our idea of space and human memory that constructs our idea of time are both fictions. They are but a kind of dream or illusion that envelopes our entire life, our being and our consciousness.

5

Unlike poets and artists, there are scientists who have, of course, warned us of how utterly wishful the human idea of the world around us has been. They tell us that it is only because we like to read all life in temporal terms, in terms of a past, present and future, that we tend to think that the Big Bang is an event that 'has been'. Had we humans not used language to articulate the idea—language that necessarily uses a past, present and a future tense—we may well have spoken of the Big Bang as an ongoing, ever present, continuing phenomenon, with us being right in the middle of it.

By the way, when, in human time, did the Big Bang happen? About 14 billion years ago. It is about four and a half billion years ago that the system of planets that we like to call 'ours' settled down to its routine of revolutions and rotations, its gravitational pulls and pushes, its balanced and reasonably predictable motion. It is a little less than two and a half billion years ago that matter started turning into life, and later, developing consciousness. And it is just about a quarter of a million years ago that an animal 'like us' became distinctly like us. This animal, *Homo sapiens*, supposedly the wisest and decidedly erect, acquired the skill of language barely 70,000 years ago, creating tenses and clocks to grasp time, and measures of distance to grasp space.

Most of the ideas of what the cosmos is, its genesis, progression and stability are not much older than 2,000 or 3,000 years, and the scientific propositions describing them—which, too, are contained within human language and thought and, therefore, conditioned by the limits of the human ability to express—are probably not over a few centuries old.

Given that the human brain is constantly evolving and, in the process, acquiring untold powers to comprehend progressively complex realities, it is but to be expected that it forces human language and thought to go beyond the established logic of tense and distance, beyond memory and imagination, beyond time and space, so that a far more complex multi-frame reality can be apprehended, understood and articulated by humans through whatever means they will in the not-so-distant future.

This is, of course, no science fantasy. It is the minimum logic of the evolutionary process of which *Homo sapiens* has been a crucial link. The signs of the 'shift' are aplenty, and this time it is not just a matter of realigning various fields of knowledge and re-drawing of disciplines. This one cannot even be adequately described by the expression 'epistemic shift', as could be said of the one in which fields of knowledge started following the Newtonian worldview in place of the previously held Ptolemaic or Aristotelian worldview. It is also not the kind of theoretical shift that involved the replacement of the *Sankhya* by the *Nyaya* School of *darshana* or philosophy. This time round, it appears that the very basis of knowledge itself is being radically transformed and refigured.

6

Neurologists explain the current shift in man's cognitive processes by pointing to the rapidly changing ways in which the brain stores and analyses sensory perceptions as well as abstract concepts and information. Linguists have raised alarm about the sinking fortunes of natural languages through which human communication has taken place over the last seven millennia. They have started noticing that the use of man-made memory chips fed into intelligent machines make heavy dents in the human ability to remember, and even in the tense patterns of natural languages.

Technologists—particularly those astride the leading glory of information and communication technology (ICT)—have been talking of network communities as a substitute for human civilisations. There is excitement in the air about the future, but there is also alarm in the minds. This is so on all fronts of knowledge, in all aspects of social organisation and all branches of human experience. Collectively, for all nations, ethnic and cultural groups, the vision of a life well beyond our imagination has started appearing on the horizon even if it has not become fully manifest, making a mockery of all that the human brain and mind have so far held as being natural and permanent.

In the new experience of the world waiting for all of us, memory as we have so far used is expected to be of little use, and imagination as we have so far exercised is predicted to be entirely transformed. The species *Homo sapiens*, it is believed, is moving out of memory, imagination and even language, and is poised to enter a post-human phase of natural evolution. Man and the intelligent machine, together, are expected to develop a new image-based system of communication, a new post-human and predominantly externalised memory and a sphere of imagination where multiple frames of existence seamlessly collide.

This image of things to come—call it utopia, call it dystopia—is profoundly unnerving, not because it involves fundamental challenges to established frames of reference and understanding; not also because our sense of beauty, ethics and truth will be entirely transformed, but because so many communities—ethnic, linguistic, cultural—and innumerable groups on the economic fringes will have to pay the cost of this transformation by facing misery, deprivation and extinction.

Just as the Industrial Revolution and the associated rise of capitalism in European countries placed the traditional agrarian society at risk, and gave rise to the long-drawn conflicts between nature and man, labour and capital, man and machine, this great transition facing us globally will create strife and, consequently, violence of an unprecedented order. This time, too, the post-human societies are likely to get divided between those with access to the digital, and those without it.

Already, some linguistic laboratories have started publishing lists of 'digitally dead languages', with over 98 per cent of Indian languages included in the list. Already, communities which are not networked are being described as 'non-civil'. Already, economies of the world seem to have resolved that citizens without unique, State-listed identities can be written off, like characters in Saadat Hasan Manto's stories, as the nowhere people. In our excitement for the utopia of a life and world 'beyond imagination', it would be tragic if we forgot the struggles and the plight of those who are on the digital fringes. Aphasia, therefore, appears to be spread out as inevitable for the future of human memory.

Notes

[1] Edward Pegler, 'Indo-European wheel words', in the web group 'Armchair prehistory: Some thoughts on human nature, past and present', on 25 May 2011.

LECTURES

3 Language Diversity*

That we were born in time and space is an absolute condition. But it is also true that time and space have been created by human beings by the use of language. While other animals live in the same space, geographical space, physical space, it is the human animal that invents a different kind of memory, memory other than what it is biologically gifted with, with the use of the past tense. When I remember today that I am the same person as I was yesterday, I am actually creating memory by the use of the past tense. Having invented, named and conceptualised memory as a device created by consciousness to integrate, to bind together different fragments of time, we start putting more colours into this new device. Other animals are not able to use memory in the same way as humans, though they do have

* Author's note: This was a lecture given on 22 November 2010 at Jnanapravaha Mumbai, for a mixed group of professionals interested in aesthetics, arts and culture. The recording of the lecture was transcribed by Professor Rupalee Burke, 20 November 2015. The edited transcription is reproduced here, with the kind permission of Dr. Rashmi Poddar, Director, Jnanapravaha, and Professor Rupalee Burke.

memory of a different kind which functions through association, but without the ability to articulate what is absent. My saying that, 'That apple I ate in Paris was fabulous' when I am neither in Paris nor eating that apple is something that other animals cannot do so far. Though we know that bees have some way of articulating, and seals perhaps, and some kinds of dolphins have some articulation, this is still very new. It is through memory that we organise time and it is through imagination that we organise our space.

Thomas Hobbes, in the eighth chapter of the *Leviathan,* talks about how the human imagination works. He says it is through the eye that images of objects enter the mind. And as if the mind were a kind of room storing all kinds of odds and things, these images, they start decaying. This process of decaying is described by Hobbes as imagination. But he misses one thing. Even other animals have eyes, and images do enter their minds; I am using the term 'mind' in a popular sense here and not in a Freudian sense. But other animals have not developed the ability to draw mental pictures or use the eyes like a camera as humans can—Wordsworth's poetry, for instance, has been called 'photographic'. Images enter in the form of pictures, but other animals are not able to reproduce or externalise these pictures. It is only the human animal that integrates image with language. Every image that enters the mind is named either nascently or in an articulate manner, either vaguely in grey colours or in black and white; and then the imagination starts functioning to help us organise space and time. It is with language that we make sense of the world. It is with language, which aids memory and imagination, that we are able to make sense of both space and time. And therefore all processes of cognition, or if not, of perception, are absolutely controlled, guided and driven by language. This is something very unique which marks us out in comparison with all other living beings. So, in other words, I can say that it is language which makes us human; therefore, it is absolutely priceless as an acquisition, as an accomplishment and as a heritage.

The next thing I want to say about language is that language is not mere expression; it is a lot more than expression. The human eyes are a very good means of expressing. Actually, the eyes are the most transparent means of expressing, for they age naturally with the body. While most other animals use the eyes to communicate, humans have chosen not the eyes but the voice to express and to communicate. Because early in their history, humans must have found the voice to be an extremely flexible means of naming things, particularly things that you cannot see. You cannot see your own back, for instance, but using voice you can name it 'the back'. This invention is probably the most fundamental of the inventions made by the human brain—I will not use the term 'mind' here—and that made a very big difference to the evolution of the species. That is, I am saying, language distinguishes us from other animals; but language also helped humans in the evolution of their species.

There is a third thing about language that we need to know. And that is, language is bound in invisible but very definite ways by the economies and human practices of production. And that therefore, the way humans related to languages when they were in the pre-hunting-gathering stage, when they were in the hunting-gathering stage, when they moved on to the pastoral stage of civilisation and from there to the agrarian, and then to the capitalistic stage in our own times, and beyond capitalistic, the way humans relate to language constantly changes. And therefore, there cannot be a 'definition' of what language is, such as what sociology offers us: language is a system. It is an arbitrary system. But it is not arbitrary in the same way in every economic phase. And I am not talking of micro-economic changes but very sweeping, macro, large-scale economic changes in human history. And therefore, the arbitrariness of the composition of language as a system keeps changing. I'll give some simple examples because this itself could be an independent lecture. In the hunting-gathering stage, humans are known to have used more of verbs and nouns and practically no adjectives. It is when they move to the pastoral stage that the adjective is invented. You look at the Vedic forms of language and the post-Vedic forms of language, and you find that it is mostly the adjective which is added as the new invention. It is with the agrarian economy that for the first time writing is invented.

Now let us dissociate ourselves from this idea that language and script are inter-related. They have logically absolutely no relationship. I'm saying there's no logical relationship between language, a given language and the script which is used for writing that language. It is the practice of putting in circulation accumulation, or surplus if you like to call it that in a very populist way. It is the practice of putting surplus in use that necessitates the use of making marks. I engage somebody to do my work and pay something in return which is surplus with me. Repeated transactions of this nature which the memory cannot hold within itself in oral form require making marks on rock or wood, and it is these marks which eventually become the first marks for vowel sounds in any language. You will notice that the numerals of a given society are fairly close in the graphic form to the vowel marks that that particular society uses in script. Since language is not the same in every economy, we will have to think of what is happening to language in our own times by placing it within our own context.

We have now come to believe that languages have, you know, some kind of main languages and dialects. This is a fairly new idea and, I would say, a debatable idea. I'll come to why it is debatable and so on. But the stratified perception of language, standard language and dialects, standard language and social use has a certain history of stratification, and we need to look at what that history has been, even if very briefly, in the given time. Week before the last I spoke on the *Mahabharata* and I mentioned, and every scholar present here mentioned, that it had several versions even at the beginning. There is Vyasa's *Mahabharata*, Janmajaya's *Mahabharata*, Shuka's *Mahabharata*, Sanjaya's *Mahabharata* and so on. And all these versions of the epic are spread over about six generations, I would say, or about 300 to 250 years, as historians and archaeologists have calculated. We know that a language undergoes fairly big changes in a matter of a century. Two centuries is a long time, and so these versions did not belong to the same language type or the same style; yet all these versions were accepted as being at par. No particular version of the *Mahabharata*, whether it was Shuka's 8,000 lines, or Sanjaya's 8,000 lines, or Ugrashava's 8,000 lines, was given greater legitimacy; there was no hierarchy of which style, which linguistic version of the *Mahabharata* was more or less important. They were all seen as being at par.

We move further down or closer to our times in history, and you notice that in *Mrichchhakatika*, there is a thief in the forest and there is a king in the city, and they speak two different languages, and I am not talking of different styles here but two languages, and within that play these two languages are accepted as being at par, as part of the same beautiful object called the *Mrichchhakatika* play. In Kalidasa's plays we have characters of the fourth century speaking in up to six different languages in the same play, and the audience had no trouble accepting all of them as being at par. When we move to the sixth century after Christ, we have the theory known as *Riti* theory which actually celebrates the idea that many languages can coexist. I will not get into the long story of *Kathasaritsagar*, but Paishachi and Sanskrit were accepted in *Kathasaritsagar* as being at par. Vishwanath in the fourteenth century composed and wrote the *Prashasti Manjari* in sixteen different languages, and Vishwanath treated all these sixteen as his languages. I'm not saying he was multilingual. I'm just saying that in the literary society of that time, there was no power hierarchy between languages. When such a hierarchy was proposed, if at all, the people rebelled against it. Eknath, the Marathi poet, had said if Sanskrit is made by gods, is Marathi made by thieves? And his audience liked that statement. Eknath was not criticising Sanskrit by making this statement. What I am trying to say is that there have been times in this country when a multitude of languages were used, but no language was seen as more important or less important than the others.

I go back a little in history once again and look at the eleventh century, the second millennium of Indian history. It is a fascinating time when new languages are taking birth, whether it is Bangla, Oriya, Kashmiri or Punjabi, Marathi or Gujarati, various tongues from which was formulated what is now known officially as Hindi; and in the South, though Tamil was older, Kannada and then of course Malayalam and Telugu. It is not that all of them evolved in the eleventh century, but beginning with the ninth or tenth century, going up to Punjabi in the fourteenth century, all these languages take birth. There is a sense of celebration about the birth of these languages. Probably in the entire cultural history of our country, the most phenomenally important cultural event is the birth of so many languages, and their sustaining themselves over a period of 1,000 years. We have not looked at them that way so far, but we need to.

During the thirteenth century, a little change—which could have become a radical change but did not and only remained a little change—started taking place. And that was, India started using paper for writing. There were many Armenian merchants in Delhi, as history tells us, who flourished by engaging in the paper trade in the thirteenth century. China had been using paper much before us. Europe, as you know, and we can forgive them, had started using paper for writing a couple of centuries later, but these things happened all the time in history. When paper came into use, one would have accepted that the spoken immediately got relegated to the background, and the written got foregrounded. That did not happen. When Eknath's *Gatha*, which was a piece of writing, was drowned, the poems in the *Gatha* survived because Tukaram, Kabir, Mira, Eknath, Namdev, Nanak, Basesvara, Tyagraja, they all sang as well as wrote their compositions; so there was no hierarchy, no distinction between what was written and what was spoken. This was the condition of Indian languages till about the eighteenth century; the written and the spoken coexisted. Even if there were clashes between different speech communities on other issues, there was no clash about the nature of speech they used, or about the languages they used. India has never known a language war in our history, I mean, until the eighteenth century or so.

It was in the eighteenth century that new ideas of what is language, how it grows, how it gets transformed started coming to us. In Germany, for example, there was a famous principle proposed. That principle is known as the 'Vowel Glide', the great shift in vowels, when there is movement from one language to another language because the way people start pronouncing their vowels changes. Instead of 'aa' you start saying 'a'; instead of 'a' you start saying 'e'; instead of 'e' you start saying 'o' or something like that. Like what we have seen with the word 'immediate'. My generation knows that word as 'immediate', and the present generation knows that word as 'ammediate'; so 'e' becomes 'a' or something like that. That is the 'Vowel Impact'. One idea floated in Germany was that the language shift happens because of this vowel glide, and thus from one language another language takes birth. Another idea—and one that really disturbs when you look at it more closely, an idea that has impacted the destiny of all people in the world without exception—was that languages grow like trees, they branch off, there's a genealogy, there is some kind of language family like the branches of a tree. So this idea was absolutely along the lines of botany. As if languages were mapped out, as if there was some common source. Umberto Eco has written a fascinating book about this, *The Search for the Perfect Language*[1]. Now we know that idea came up because of the other philosophical trappings of that time, because all knowledge was seen as knowledge of one kind and anything that was inconsistent with the rest of the knowledge was not seen as knowledge—it became *non-knowledge*. Therefore, in the field of linguistics, too, there was this 'oneness' or conformity which became the centre of all investigations and therefore, all languages all over the world were seen as if they belonged to the great Indo-Aryan family or the Indo-European family or the Indo-Iranian family. And so this idea of the oneness of all languages started being used to describe languages.

In reality, however, this is not how Indians had looked at their own languages. Indians have had very sophisticated philosophies of language right through. Whether it was Panini, or Bhartrihari, or Katyayana, many philosophers had devoted thought to language in the *Vaisheshikas*. If you read B. K. Matilal's books you will see what a sophisticated and complex philosophy of language several Indian traditions had developed, including the Jaina tradition which Matilal does not discuss. D. R. Nagraj had begun work on the Jaina tradition and attempted to recover medieval texts in Kannada, particularly Jaina texts, under the caption 'Recovering Memory' around 1995, but unfortunately his project never came to completion due to his early death. Then, at the beginning of the nineteenth century, for the first time some Indian languages were printed. Though one printing machine had accidentally gone from Portugal to Goa, it did not work for very long. It was used for a while for printing Kannada, but did not have any runs beyond a point. It was in the last quarter of the eighteenth century that the first Marathi book was printed; the first Gujarati book was printed. Then at the beginning of the nineteenth century, at St. Fort Williams, Lallujilal was appointed by the Company Sarkar, and he started printing books in Indian languages.

Now which Indian languages did Lallujilal select for printing books? Were these languages that had scripts? Not necessarily, because in India many scripts were used for writing one language, and one script used for writing many languages. For example, Sanskrit was written in two or three different scripts. The Devanagari script was used for many languages. The Modi script was used for writing practically every language, whether southern or northern. So Lallujilal did not have any rational basis for the selection of languages when they were printed. Languages were printed keeping in mind, say, how Mukesh Ambani distributes agencies for sale of oil. Lallujilal saw the administrative convenience of the Company Sarkar and accordingly chose languages for the purpose of printing. Obviously, when works in these languages were printed, Indians, who felt at ease with any language and any form of language whether written or spoken, picked up printing as a new addition to the range of amazing language skills they had acquired, and started writing rather than just composing. So during the nineteenth century there is a kind of effervescence, occasionally described as the 'Renaissance', when language and literature became the driving engine for social change.

Sadly, this situation resulted in something very tragic when we approach Independence. And that is, if you look at the Constitution of India, all the debates about the great social and political issues, issues of rights, entitlement, land-holding and various others, all the issues that were resolved resulted in the writing of Articles of the Constitution; and all the issues which were unresolved resulted in the writing of the Schedules of the Constitution. These are still open debates—whether it is the

Schedule on tribes or the Schedule on caste—because we do not really know how to look at these questions in the context of modern India. So the Constitution created a Schedule on languages, with a footnote which said that this Schedule is also not concluded as a Schedule, let alone as an Article! So the question of Indian languages was left completely inconclusive and unresolved, and language was probably among the most difficult, most ticklish of the inconclusive debates that the Constituent Assembly and the thinkers before the Constituent Assembly was constituted had to face. Gandhi had tried to deal with it in some ways, but we'll take that up later maybe in our discussion.

The Schedule on languages had 14 languages. Now which 14 languages were put there? Languages that had printed literature in them. Which languages had printed literature in them? The ones that Lallujilal had chosen at St. Fort Williams. They had nothing to do with literary development, or linguistic richness, or the number of speakers, or the geographical area covered by a language. These were irrational decisions that history brought to our doorstep when the Constitution got accepted by the people of India. And after Independence it became binding on the Government of India, whenever it spends that mandatory amount on education, to spend for education in the languages listed in the Constitution. Therefore, all the other languages had no patronage. These other languages did not require patronage specifically. But since the country had accepted the institutionalisation of education for promoting knowledge and taking it to the next generation, education was therefore institutionalised by some languages. And in that context only some languages got empowered, and the others started languishing.

Now what is the number of such languages that languish? We know that in the Eighth Schedule today there are 22 languages, so 22 is a large number. You tell a Frenchman or a German, 22 languages are supported by the Central government. When the government writes to UNESCO, they write that we promote education in 22 languages, we have radio in 40 languages, we have printing in 65 languages. UNESCO gets duly impressed. So if you look at the other languages which are not on radio, not printed, not supported for education, in the 1961 Census, the citizens of India wrote that they spoke a total of 1,652 mother-tongues. Now please remember that every mother-tongue is not necessarily a language. I might jolly well say that my mother-tongue is the Advanced Studies language, but it will not become a language. Mother-tongues will have to be examined and linguists will have to see if the claims are for real, because Sindhi is claimed under 20 different names as Bharuchi Sindhi, Amdavadi Sindhi, Puna Sindhi, Gandhinagar Sindhi, because wherever Sindhis settle, the townships are named as Gandhinagar and so on. But it is one language. However, even these verified claims amount to nearly 1,100 or more. Not all mother-tongues could actually be verified in the interim period between any two censuses of this country because ten years is too small a period to do that. Incidentally, language is a subject with the Ministry of Home Affairs in our country, not the Ministry of Education, and the Registrar General's office would not have the vast task force needed to check and validate all these claims. Even so, there are approximately 1,100 mother-tongues or so.

Ten years later in 1971 when the census was conducted and the statistics were released in 1976, six years later because it takes that much time, something terrible had happened outside India. In 1972, Pakistan split up and Bangladesh became what it is now on the question of language. And that really frightened the census authorities and they decided that they would not release the entire statistics but introduce a cut-off point. And they said that if a certain language is written as mother-tongue by more than 10,000 people, then they would put it in the list. As a result the 1970 list had only 109 names in the list of languages. Now please remember that these were not 109 languages: the 109th was, it read in the list, all 'the others'. The others were those 1,500 languages which were pushed under the carpet. After Independence, until 1971 at least the names of mother-tongues were reflected in the Census of India. After 1971, even the names of languages of, say, the Wadars, the Madaris, the Sansis were all wiped out. It is a kind of a punishment. People who speak these languages are punished by the State, and the only term that can be used to describe this punishment is that their tongues are clipped. The term from the Greek language is *aphasia*. They are punished with speechlessness because their speech has become illegitimate, unsupported, unviable, and a burden for the development project in this country.

There is one argument often put forward: why do we have to have all these languages? Can we really sustain them? Is it possible to run this country as one country if we have all these languages? And these questions have their source in a certain faulty idea of nationalism—what is a nation—which is of course of European origin, because they have one people, often one religion, and one language. And we have also come to believe that only through the medium of English can India modernise itself and be on equal terms, equal footing with the rest of the world. Please remember that in the Parliament of India, almost 97 per cent of Indian languages were never heard. If you understand a language as a worldview, language as a means of organising your space and time, language as a means of naming everything outside the consciousness and therefore a worldview, it means that 97 per cent of India's worldviews are not reflected in the body which makes decisions for 100 per cent of Indians. So we are using 3 per cent worldviews to decide for 100 per cent Indians. Possibly, it explains the vast rift between the political class and the people of India which is noticed again and again, not only at the time of elections when people don't turn up to vote but again and again the kind of hatred, unjustified hatred, and I am speaking on behalf of the politicians, I am trying to defend them, not each one of them is a villain, not each one of them is a crook, you know, borrowed from the Hollywood films. Most of them are very sensible people and very knowledgeable persons, but they are hated by the people of India because the percentage of worldviews used in Indian development, Indian planning, Indian decision-making is very, very disproportionately small compared to the percentage of worldviews that prevail in the country. Why has there not been any policy to take into account this very big asset that India has?

During the Eleventh Five Year Plan, the Government of India set up a small committee to think of the growth of the non-Scheduled languages. I was asked to chair that committee, prepare a report. The Planning Commission accepted that report. The Ministry accepted the money set aside by the Planning Commission, several hundred crore rupees, and created a Bharat Bhasha Vikas Yojana. This Yojana had some 16 features. When the Ministry wanted to implement this Yojana, it found that it could not because they did not have an official list of languages. They know that the country has so many languages, they have heard about it from newspapers, magazines, people like me; but they do not have on record an official list of languages. The last such list, and we are not talking of the census, we are talking of the survey: the census is what the citizens claim, the survey is a report going out from the Central Institute of Indian Languages or some such institute, it is different. The last known comprehensive survey was carried out by George Grierson, who was an Irish scholar. Because he was Irish he did not rise up in the British official hierarchy and so he felt a bit discriminated against even though he was working for the British here. Therefore he decided he would focus more on his language studies rather than running the country for the British, and so from his very early years in India he started publishing grammars of Bihari languages and so on and then he undertook a linguistic survey of India; part of it was conducted from Shimla itself. I am sure his office must be somewhere here and we must locate where it is someday. Grierson found out there are 189 languages, and about 544 dialects. Many languages which are languages were treated by him as dialects. Many languages he simply could not cover. The Nizam of Hyderabad did not give him easy access, and so the languages of that area were left out. The languages of the nomadic communities were more or less completely left out because the nomadic communities were themselves seen as stigmatised, criminal communities by the British government, and often they were actually asked to stay in settlements outside the cities and towns, and they wrongly came to be known as 'criminal tribes'. So Grierson did not have much access to such communities, or he did not think it necessary to include their languages. But even with all those defects, his was probably the last comprehensive survey of languages in the country.

Another attempt was made in the South and a survey of languages in Tamil Nadu was carried out. There were surveys of specific states carried out. The division of Indian states was linguistic. But even today we do not have an official list of languages in a country where states, politically empowered states, were created on the basis of language. The result is that a huge amount of wisdom is lost for this country. I was doing the survey of Himalayan languages, and I found there are 162 terms for snow in all the Himalayan languages together. There is a term for snow that falls on a river, for snow that falls on clear water, different terms. Now suppose the rivers of the Himalayas rise because the Himalayas are melting at a rate higher than they ought to. If the rivers overflow and flood the rest of Bangladesh, Burma, India and Pakistan, or if they dry up altogether causing serious havoc, which are predictions, we will perhaps hire experts from Israel or Japan to tell us how to deal with all this rather than looking at these languages which have traditional wisdom, ecological wisdom in them. It is known that when the tsunami hit the Andamans, the Adivasis there knew how to protect themselves because in their languages there are terms of ecological wisdom.

Today most people are not able to meet a doctor in their own language. Our anaesthetists have become anglicised, and therefore, our aesthetics, too. These two are closely related—anaesthetics is management of pain; aesthetics is management of pleasure. Both these terms were coined by the Greeks. The Greeks were overwhelmingly, obsessively interested in how shadows are created, and therefore they always thought of the world of light and the world of darkness together when they composed their languages. You know that Derrida begins his discussion on language by quoting a Greek term which simultaneously means both medicine and poison. The Greeks wanted to create shadows in words. Hence, I am trying to say that in India patients are not able to meet doctors in their mother-tongues; children are not able to speak with their mothers in their mother-tongues. And as a result a huge amount of wisdom accumulated in these languages is lost. I am not trying to validate or eulogise or praise everything that is traditional. Please do not mistake me for a Hindu nationalist or any such—that is not the project that I have. But a language is earned through hard labour. Unless you have the experience of fatigue, physical experience of fatigue, you will not be able to coin the word; a language does not coin the word fatigue. It is on the basis of long human experiences, over many generations, that words are coined. And when words are lost, those experiences are lost, too. I think the condition of Indian languages today is alarming. And this is not just for the poor and tribal people whose languages are denied and therefore no dialogue with the Adivasis is possible in our country today. But this is also a very big problem for academics and intellectuals in this country. If we accept, and there should be no difficulty in accepting this, that language is the only means of mental transaction, if we accept that a language supports, just as a table supports so many things, papers and cups and mikes, a language supports wider cognitive concepts. Then if we are working on these cognitive concepts, cognitive categories, if we are trying to make these cognitive categories operative or invent new categories, and if we did not have the basis of a pool of languages available to us, possibly our intellectual class shall never be able to contribute anything original. The best they can do is to make excellent copies, but nothing original in the world of knowledge.

The question is, can a person not work in a foreign language? The answer is yes, an individual can. Joseph Conrad could, Sri Aurobindo and Jawaharlal Nehru could. An individual can. But an entire speech community moving to a new speech habitat is a great loss. We are now in a kind of situation which is cyclical, and it is a vicious cycle where people do not speak the languages used in schools and universities. They remain either so-called 'illiterate' or so-called 'underdeveloped' people, and because they are illiterate and underdeveloped they cannot have access to better education and come out of that. The next thing I want to mention is that our literacy figures, despite huge efforts by the Sarva Shiksha Abhiyan, are still showing somewhere at 70 per cent. Please remember that 30 per cent of the people whose languages are denied, they are not necessarily illiterate, but they are not able to relate to other languages. And so if we continue with this kind of language rift then the future for this country is not very bright. So in order to preserve our knowledge stock, in order to make our country more democratic, in order that the parliamentary decision-making reflects all worldviews, we will have to look at the language question very seriously. In order to do that, I have started doing a people's linguistic survey, a listing of all possible languages in the country in a measurably limited time. Obviously the government is not interested in supporting any such venture because the Home Ministry feels very worried about this. And so I am working with the help of funds raised by Adivasis in Gujarat or individual donations and with the help of community cultural activists all over the country. I am very happy to say that about 16 volumes will be ready by the end of 2012. And after Grierson we will once again have a list of Indian languages which we need to respect. I think I have said what I have to say so I will stop. Thank you.

Notes

[1] Umberto Eco, *The Search for the Perfect Language*, translated from the Italian by James Fentress (Oxford: Blackwell, 1995).

4 Aesthetics for Our Time

The Ashok Ranade Memorial Lecture*

Ladies and gentlemen, we lost Dr. Ashok Ranade too, too soon. This is actually the time we should have been listening to him, learning from him. The kind of intellectual giant that he was with the versatility he had and the very deep understanding of cultural changes that he showed. His not being with us has created a vacuum which is not filled and may not be filled anytime soon. This is the time when we needed him all the more that he is not with us. If I accepted to speak, it is out of my gratitude to him as a student of literature and culture. I did not get an opportunity of meeting him personally, but I knew of the framework that you referred to, and in fact for this evening I have chosen out of that framework a very small component. Of all the books that he wrote—because my access to him was through books, and I read Marathi as well as English—one

---

* Author's note: A memorial lecture instituted by students and friends of Dr. Ashok Ranade, this was delivered on 10 December 2013 at the National Centre for Performing Arts, Mumbai. The recording of the lecture was transcribed by Professor Rupalee Burke. An edited version of the transcription is reproduced here.

that struck me as a book very close to my own concerns was on ethno-musicology. He would not have liked to use the term 'ethno-musicology' which he had contested almost 15 years before he wrote that book. He did not write the book; it came as a series of lectures, the two Prof. Karnik Memorial Lectures he gave which were subsequently published in 1992, and in this book he details how ethno-musicology fed into the Indology project of the British of understanding India—understanding with quotation marks—and in a way, devastating India. At the beginning of those two lectures he raised many very pertinent questions, questions which have been asked but not fully answered over the last two centuries.

Dr. Ranade begins by asking what happens when two cultures come together and particularly when one of those is dominant and the other a dominated culture? Is it that the dominated culture automatically accepts everything from the dominating culture? Is it that certain strategies are evolved? Is it that what emerges as a result of it is an understanding that is not perfect but necessary? He raises several questions and he tries to show how the project of ethno-musicology that the British undertook with regard to India was a companion project to their project of Indology which was trying to understand India in a way that was congenial to their imagination and their sense of memory, and not a graph or graphic or snapshot of what India actually was. The conclusion of that book is fantastically insightful, but I will mention it when I conclude what I have to say.

So, what happens when two cultures come together in a situation of combat or sometimes in a situation of complicity or of collaboration or of conflict? Of course, as Dr. Ranade reminds us, this is not the first time this has happened in India and the history of such cultural clashes and collaborations in India is very long, and for him, India is a spectrum and not a spot. India has many and not one culture or tradition, and that is a remarkably realistic view of Indian traditions or set of traditions. And for want of a convenient English term, I will use the word tradition whereas I should have been saying several or hundreds of traditions and so on, as Dr. Ranade would like me to do.

The question of aesthetics for the contemporary Indian arts has to be seen in the context of those traditions or that tradition; it has to be seen in the context of the historical experience of the combat or the complicity between clashing cultures; but if I may mention here that the term 'aesthetics' is no longer fashionable. If I were to go back to the university which I left some time back, nobody would admit me if I were to say that I want to discuss aesthetics. That is no longer a fashionable term in academic discourse. It is a term of nineteenth-century origin. It gained currency and immense popularity in the nineteenth century, and a certain fallout of that popularity reflected in the Indian situation in the first half of the twentieth century, until B. S. Mardhekar's times or maybe Prof. R. B. Patankar's times. But I'll use this term 'aesthetics' nonetheless for want of another term which will serve my purpose.

Now aesthetics, like history, is a problem term. I mean, history is both a course of events and also a narrative about that course of events. So you have the history of science, that's what departments of history do, and then there is a history that people like say Akbar or Rana Pratap or Shivaji or Gandhi or Nelson Mandela made. Aesthetics pertains to what is there in the things which we generally think are beautiful, but it also specifies our response to all those things. Fortunately, there is a little bit of convenience, that is we can use the term 'aesthetic' when it pertains to performance, production, expression, and also 'aesthetics' as in 'linguistic' and 'linguistics,' 'aesthetics' for our response to those things.

Now aesthetics is based in language. Let me explain. The history of human language is just about 70,000 years. Prior to that we did not use full sentences. Therefore, the history of creativity in language is a little shorter than that period of 70,000 years. In the course of those thousands of years, humans were not necessarily aware that they were creating something extraordinary by way of poetry or theatre or dance or music. That awareness enters the human consciousness only through a very fundamental, phenomenal economic change, and that is the rise of agrarian societies all over the world about 10,000 years or 8,000 years before our time. It is when the value of production enters human thought. Until then, like the dance of honeybees, the art of human beings was not art at all, it was life; and, as Marx would say, 'industrial workers separate work and life'. Humans did not separate art and life. Life was art, art was life. This problem has remained with us till our times. Just about 200 years ago Edmund Burke had to break his head thinking of how to sort this out and he said, 'Well, those things in arts are beautiful but those things which we think are beautiful but cannot be called arts are sublime'. So art became restricted as a form, as a manner, as a style of expression with the rise of language and with the rise of a certain economic order in society.

Style of expression came much later. The earliest records of reflection on the manner or style of expression or the content of expression or why expression at all on the arts, whether it is music, dance, theatre, poetry, whatever, dates back to fairly recent times, just about 2,500 years old. In Greece we find this emerging about 2,000 years ago. On our side, if we were to take *Tolkappiyam*, or Bharatamuni, the contemporary of *Tolkappiyam* in Sanskrit as the beginner of this task, this great enterprise of thinking about the arts dates to about 2,000 years. The aesthetics developed by Aristotle or Socrates or Plato, even if Plato did not like the arts very much, or that developed by Bharatamuni or in the *Tolkappiyam*, whoever is the author of *Tolkappiyam* in Tamil, was the aesthetics of thinking about the arts, and their business was to look at what binds various forms of arts whether it is music, dance, literature, theatre, poetry or whatever they call arts, to look at what is the basic semology, what is the moving principle that makes us express. The Greeks use the term '*vets*' for the inspired poets; we use the term *ojas* for being touched by some divine energy like a mad person. But the difference was that the Greeks thought of the thing produced, the thing that came out as art which represented a certain reality which preceded that art, a kind of perfect world, a world of ideas or ideals as the Greeks thought of it.

The ancient Greeks had a very strange view of this world. It was like this theatre. For them the stars were like holes in the sky, and above the sky there was permanent light. And in that world of permanent light there were no shadows. And shadow is death. And since there were no shadows there, they believed that nothing there dies. And therefore they felt you don't have to create many tables but one table is enough. You don't have to create many songs but one song is enough. So that one table, that one song in the world of permanent light became perfections, 'ideas'. That was the Greek sense of idea. So Greek aesthetics was trying to figure out how art—the representation of things—was seen as imperfection, as copies, how it deviated from the perfect ideas. Sometimes they argued that actually art endows something very special to those things created and therefore makes them a little better than the ideal things. But generally the view held then was that all representation is inadequate, imperfect. And therefore one needs to represent again and again till one creates a perfect representation closest to the ideal. That was the basis of Greek aesthetics.

On our side, we didn't get into the question of the thing itself or the creation. We thought that creation was an expression of divinity because the *kavi*, the poet, is a mere vehicle of a divine idea or thought or experience or a nameless thing; and therefore whether it is poetry, dance, theatre, sculpture, painting, or anything created, the question if it is perfect or imperfect does not arise. What can be perfect or imperfect is only our consciousness, and we have a huge amount of philosophy on this inadequacy of the human consciousness which results into *avidya* sometimes, which results into *vimudhta* sometimes, which results in loss of memory sometimes. All kinds of religious, philosophical and aesthetics texts have talked about how we, the perceivers, have to cultivate our consciousness, how the *rasika* has to become *sahrudaya*. Sahrudaya is not just being empathetic; it needs to be translated in the light of another expression which comes up in relation to *Natyashastra,* and that is *kavita. Kavya* is the *sahodara* of *Brahmananda,* born of the same joy that you have in the discovery of the divine. That is the sense in which the term *sahodara* or sahrudaya is used. And therefore one has to be like the poet, one has to *be* the poet, one has to wipe out the duality between the poet and oneself, and that is how we respond to music in this country even today. When I go on nodding my head to good music, it's not because I have a problem or I have no words to express my response to the music, but because I am wiping out, effacing my personality in order to try and get under the skin of the singer, be one with the music—music wipes out the difference between the singer and the listener. That was the basis of our aesthetics. But please let's not forget that the idea of literature, the idea of music, the idea of dance, the idea of drama, the idea of painting, they keep changing every few generations. What one generation describes as poetry, five generations later it can become something else. It might become *mahakavya,* it might become *itihasa,* or *smruti,* or *shruti,* or *bhakti,* or folk song. There is no one single permanent idea of what is art, or the arts, which will remain fixed forever till the end of the world. These ideas keep changing, and they must, and they change primarily because of economic reasons which lead to cultural changes and so on.

Briefly, if I have to run through these changes, on the Western side there was this idea of Aristotle, I'm referring to Aristotle's *Poetics*, the idea of representation, imperfect, inadequate representation, or representation which somehow tries to make things a little better and brings them closer to the ideal. This changes as soon as the idea of the cosmos undergoes a change. When the idea that the universe is like a box was dropped and it came to be accepted that, well somehow the universe seems to be cyclical, circular, it seems to be moving, somehow the planets are in motion, immediately they drop Aristotle, and Ptolemy's world takes over, and instead of talking about arts making things better, arts are put to the service of making human beings better. Arts become didactic rather than only mimetic, rather than copying something now they also instruct readers, listeners, audiences and so on. This is an epistemic change and with that the economics of the times changes, the philosophy changes, the law changes, the method of education changes, everything, all disciplines change. It is like the building blocks of knowledge go through a radical change. And so you have different kinds of knowledge-building again. Aesthetics is one of those; so aesthetics also changes. And when Ptolemy becomes outdated and you have again a Copernicus, a Newton, a Galileo kind of idea of the world, you have some hesitation in going entirely by Ptolemy's idea. And you move a little further, you get into a Romantic, an expressive idea of the arts, that arts must express because there is a universe within you and unless that universe is expressed, what you express does not become art. So you have the mimetic arts, didactic arts some 1,100 or 1,200 years later, and another 800 years later there is once again an epistemic change and you move into what is romantic, what is expressive and must be expressed literally, something that is there in your heart which has to be pressed out. Like the fellow who is much abused by being taught too much in our classrooms, Wordsworth said,

'Poetry is the spontaneous overflow of powerful feelings'. So it must overflow like a water tank.

On our side, too, the ideas of literature, poetry, drama, dance, music kept changing. Of course, we have Bharatamuni's *Natyashastra* as the pole star, and we must always start learning the *mudras* and *chinnhas* and *bhavas* from there with reference to that text, but that's the nature of a practice, a tradition. But what Bharatamuni was saying is that the inadequate consciousness of humans cannot understand the work that divinity inspires in poets. If you want to understand it, please break it down into smaller components. Instead of experiencing, grasping the entire play, please try to understand its different *rasas*: this is *hasya rasa*, this is *shringara rasa*, this is *shoka rasa*. This breaking down into smaller units was not an autopsy or post-mortem of a work of art, but to help our consciousness, to aid our understanding. For we can then slowly relish and talk about the *shringara* in one play, the *hasya* in another and so on and recount and experience it again and again, until our consciousness is able to become one with the poet's consciousness, the singer's consciousness, and there is no distinction between the two. Then we have Dandin, of course, who presages the *ritis* and says don't break down poetry into rasas, break it down into styles, regional styles at that. So what was a psychological metaphor for Bharatamuni—the mind of the audience—Dandin actually translates into a literal geographical metaphor, the different ritis, and he had many followers. Beginning with Dandin, going to Matanga of *Brihaddeshi* in probably the fourteenth century, a distance of almost eight or nine centuries, this geographical breakdown of styles kept happening in our country.

Then comes Anandvardhan, a very talented and gifted aesthetician. By then the *Manu Samhita* had set in and become deeply entrenched and social fragmentation had taken place irreversibly in terms of caste and in terms of unpardonable exogamy. Endogamy was made the law of society. Anandvardhan does not talk about endogamy or *Manu Samhita* but he does talk about levels of meaning in terms of a hierarchy: there's a superficial meaning, a hidden meaning, then there's yet another further up, the highest kind of meaning. Then we have Kuntak who is once again trying to look at the text.

It is with Abhinavagupta, the scholar from Kashmir, that Indian aesthetics goes through an epistemic change. Till Abhinavagupta's times all those who followed Bharata have taken Bharata's meaning but used it differently in the context of their social orders. It is Abhinavagupta who tries to synthesise things into a grand unified whole, bringing in Buddha and Krishna, *nyaya* and the contemporary philosophy of *tantra;* he was in fact a great scholar of *tantra*. Abhinavagupta tried to synthesise things to the extent that he decided not to see any distinctions at all which Bharata had so meticulously established 900 or 1,000 years before. For Abhinavagupta drama and poetry were not just at par, they were the same and with rasas. He refused to accept that flaws can occur in the poet's conception of a subject and temporarily stop the flow of the divine inspiration. He said if all of us are made of the divine stuff, if all of us are *Brahm,* if all of us are *tat,* the indescribable 'that which is', then there is no question of our not understanding. Abhinavagupta was said to be not just a poet but also a great singer.

Between the eleventh and the seventeenth century, there were many schools of thought that came up in India: the *Bhakti* schools beginning with the Shaiva cults in the south spreading to the north, going through the Maharashtra of Gnaneshwar and subsequently Eknath and Tukaram, and in Kashmir, Shaivism blossoming into other forms of joy and ecstasy, and Sufism coming in at various stages.

In Bharata's *Natyashastra,* unity was the main principle. It was based on the idea of unity between humans and the divine, and achieving that perfect unity was the aim of the arts. In Abhinavagupta's aesthetics, continuity was the basic principle in many ways. In Bhakti poetry, Bhakti performances, Bhakti theatre, Bhakti music, subjectivity was the principle, and in that neither God nor man was perfect. And both could get into a dialectic where God could become subjective, not just remain the objective, invisible, *tat*, *Brahman*, permanent, forever, indescribable, but God could take a human form, maybe a buffalo or a pillar like in Pandharpur or a lover or whatever, and the *bhaktas* would then crave for that appearance. For the bhaktas there was no distinction between art and life. The episteme had changed. For Tukaram, his bhakti was not a profession or a business or an NGO—it was with him, in him, all the time, it was everything for him. Even when the manuscripts of his songs and poems were drowned in the river Indrani, Bhakti still spread from one end of the country to the other and it continued, and in that continuity which Abhinavagupta had made possible, subjectivity was foregrounded. Now these are epistemic changes, and the idea of arts changed, in the Western tradition as well as in ours. No idea of art is permanent. Art has permanence because it has transcendence, but no idea of art has permanence.

When the British arrived in India, we encountered the Western tradition coming to us through some of the best British minds. We encountered the Romantic generation when English was introduced in India as a language of education. Had we got the English language a 100 years before, probably all our creativity would have been finished. This encounter still left us with some space because they came very close, the closest to the Indian way of perceiving things. But this was the colonial encounter, and in a colonial encounter one of the two major things that happen is that the imagination of the colonised gets truncated. For me imagination is not my ability to see dreams; that is hallucination. Imagination is not imagining things because that is about 'lies'.

Imagination in Hobbes' terms is how images of objects enter through the eye and come to rest in the brain and get processed. Now what happens to the eye with the help of the objects is actually pure physics, optics; it allows us to grasp space. If there were no objects and no light, there would be no space at all. We grasp space through imagination. The imagination gets truncated because the dominated culture has no mastery over its own space; and that mastery is made virtual. Like we had so many *rajas* and *raosahebs* and *raisahebs*, but it was nobody's call to decide about the land, land ownerships, land titles and so on. So as a result of the colonial encounter, the imagination got truncated. The second of those two things is that the memory of the colonised was affected.

Let me first say that there is no time; in this world there is no thing called time. I have sparrows in my garden; they have no time. My dog at home, I have one and I love it, it has no time. We have created time because of the way the human mind is engaged with language and which at one stage, about 30,000 years before our time, imagined the past tense and we started referring to things absent. Like yesterday I had a blue shirt on. We devised a way of telling lies, in a way, talking about non-present, non-real things. Because of the past tense we became capable of envisioning time, thinking of time, and once we created time we had to create memory, not just individual memory but even memory as a public existence. All the work that universities in the world are doing is carrying that public memory forward, giving it validity, whether it actually deserves it or not. I'm now talking of communal or community memory that goes beyond one's ken, one's limits and so on. So first we imagine time and then in order to control time, to regulate time, we develop memory as a way of connecting ourselves with others, with God, with the land, with the earth. As I was talking about those two things that colonial domination affects, one was about how the imagination gets truncated, and then one can get into some kind of euphoria of the fabulous space to come in the future, as we see in Bankimchandra's *Anandmath*. And the second thing is that the memory gets twisted and a thing called amnesia, cultural amnesia is introduced. Now please remember—I'm sorry, I want to talk about loss of memory, so I cannot say please remember—amnesia is not wiping out of memory. Amnesia, as Freud describes, is a selective way of remembering only certain things, and not remembering certain things.

The British told us, 'visit the Asiatic debates in Calcutta of 1780s' and Sir William Jones in his very first lecture says, 'I shall talk about India from the eleventh century', that is from the very beginning, from the *Vedas*—he thought that was the beginning—to the seventeenth century, but not beyond that because beyond that is all decline, degradation. If they had not held the view that from the eleventh century onward to the seventeenth century India declined, there was no justification for their coming here and ruling us. So they had to have that view. Actually from the eleventh century to the eighteenth century is an absolutely fascinating time in the cultural history of any country in the world. This is when we created new languages, Bangla, Assamese, Marathi, Kannada; Kannada is now considered a classical language; Marathi is also on the way to be considered classical. Eleventh century onwards new Indian languages sprung up, new creativity, new arts, new episteme of aesthetics; but William Jones said decline. We accepted that version that medieval India was all bad, and some of them rabid sectarians felt that it became bad because some polluting forces came in and so on. That was even worse. And some of it was tacitly encouraged by the kind of terminology that was used by Halhead, Jones and other people and the nineteenth-century British administrators.

Amnesia made us cultivate a very poor self-view. We felt that all the good that happened was in the Sanskrit tradition, which in any case Indians had given up long time back. They had not forgotten it, they revered it, they respected it, but eighteenth-century Bombaywallahs did not converse in Sanskrit. They conversed in Warli or Konkani or Parsi or Gujarati. Sanskrit had gone. But we thought, Oh! India was glorious then, wasn't it, that was the golden age, but the last 1,000 years are bad. Because of cultural amnesia we also accepted the view that whatever comes from the West is necessarily good. At one time William Jones attempted to write the score for Indian music. He tried to make oral Indian music written music. Thank goodness his efforts did not go beyond a point, and we could wait till Bhakandeji came along and did something wonderfully good to Indian music. But with literature we accepted that the Western novel is better than the *Kathasaritsagar*. I mean I don't mind appreciating Dickens, I don't mind appreciating Hardy or Wordsworth, Tennyson, Arnold. I have no quarrel, I just love those books. My unease is with the fact that in India we developed a lopsided view of ourselves, our arts, our literature, and the worst among the opinions we brought in was that unfortunately Indians have not developed aesthetics. In literature they all said for almost a 100 years that India does not have literary criticism, everything else is okay. But there's no literary criticism. So there must be something inadequate in the Indian mind, Indian personality and so on. We forgot the fact that for a 1,000 years our poets decided that literary criticism is trash, it is not necessary. Foregrounding subjectivity is necessary, not foregrounding the text and textuality.

We had the resistance movement, the nationalist movement and a due sense of pride in our traditions, sometimes excessive pride. Some of us decided to go to the West to get many good things. Some of us decided to go to the past to get many good things. And we had a mumbo-jumbo of a very strange kind of hackneyed combination of good things from all over the past and the West, but not from here. We have inherited this. In the twentieth century many very capable minds tried to counter this. I'll give two or three examples. I begin with Sri Aurobindo, a man of extraordinary brilliance, great insights, but he felt that if India deserves a new aesthetic it must be along the lines of the idea of *mantra*. The idea of mantra that Aurobindo proposed was not like the idea of *kavita* that probably Valmiki or Bharatamuni had of literature. For Aurobindo, kavita was a means of ascension to a higher level of consciousness. He felt that when one uses poetry as a means of ascension to a higher level of consciousness the world will perhaps be a better place. I'm not trying to trivialise his views; he spent almost 40 years developing them. He had a great mastery of Greek, Latin, French, English and Sanskrit literature. He was not writing light-heartedly or casually. It was not a research paper submitted for a peer-review, it was serious stuff. But Aurobindo wanted to bring in Romantic poetry, Romantic literature and infuse them with the mantra kind of inspiration, and that would be the poetry of the future. When I say Romantic poetry, it has nothing to do with the romance that we see in the films produced in this city of Bombay; it's a technical term with which many of you are familiar. Aurobindo wrote a book, a series of essays which he allowed to be compiled and published towards the end of his life when he was seventy-eight, a very mature *yogi*. The book is called *The Future Poetry*. He was trying to seek a synthesis of an older tradition and a distant future tradition.

A couple of decades later comes Anand Coomaraswamy, another great man. Rarely has such erudition, such eclecticism been combined with such generosity of spirit. Because for him Greek thought, ancient Sanskrit thought, pre-ancient Egyptian thought, tenth-century Chinese thought and sixteenth-century Japanese thought could all sit comfortably together. Coomaraswamy believed in a kind of perennial thought which manifests itself in all thoughts in the world at all times. This goes against the very grain of what thought is and how it secures itself in language and how that language, and therefore thought, functions in the human consciousness—neurologically, psychologically, philosophically and historically. We then had B. S. Mardhekar here in Maharashtra who was greatly taken up by the idea of aesthetics, and for him the work of Benedetto Croce—the British were already used by then but not the Italians—was a novelty. Mardhekar was brilliant in his modernist poetry in Marathi, he was a good novelist, an experimentalist, but in aesthetics he somehow missed the point.

I think it is at that point that Ashokji's contribution is very significant. Towards the end of his book on ethno-musicology, he says one thing that India proves is that diversity is far more important for us than any unity brought about through coercion or domination, and therefore we know how to keep it alive. This is an extraordinary thought for our times, I think. Because we are arrested in a web of traditions which we have inherited—both from the past and from the West—and which we obviously should not and cannot give up. But these traditions cannot all sit together comfortably, because their origin is in this attitude of making imperfect creations, cosmic cyclicity, the urge to express oneself, not the divine self but oneself, which is very different from these ideas of the perceiver's mind being inadequate, or a great continuity of experience alone making you capable of singing as well as listening, or this great subjectivity which the *bhaktas* brought to bear upon all expressions. These are all philosophically, logically disparate; they cannot be welded together in terms of their thought structure. It is like you can make an alloy by bringing many metals together, but you cannot possibly put both sugar and chilly in water to make it either sweet or hot. They do it in *bhelpuri* and *panipuri*, but I don't know how that is done. (Dr. Devy makes a slurping sound much to the delight of the audience.)

The concluding paragraph of Dr. Ranade's book is titled 'Diversity Alone'. Now let me say something about this. The British not only left our imagination truncated and our cultural memory twisted—or rather, they did not do anything but we did it because of their presence; they were far too busy and not so numerous as we were, but it happened to us—not just that but they also segmented our society. The story of how the criminal tribes were created in this country is mindboggling. It is worse than what happened to the Jews in Germany. From 1871 onwards a wrongly crafted Act segmented certain communities, declaring them criminal by birth, segregating them, keeping them within fences, making them do hard labour, until 1952 when they were denotified—190 communities; today there are about six to seven crore people. The British also segmented us by creating a sector called 'tribes' because the forest land had to be taken over by the Sovereign Crown. The forests in India were brought under the sovereign domain by law and those living in the forests were told that this is not your land; you go wherever you want or be subservient to us. In essence, that is the story. The social segmentation did not stop at just creating the criminal people, the forest people, the denotified people, the crafts people; some of them were performers, *kolatis*, the Baul singers, *madaris*, makers of musical instruments and so on. They also segmented us by creating a cartography of language and society. Grierson did a great job of the language survey, but when he encountered about 700 samples he quickly put 189 in one basket, saying these are good languages, full languages, and all the others are dialects. So a dialect is a little less than a language; that is like saying, you are okay, you are also alive but not a complete human being as such. So that shows the British cartographic mindset. They carried out the social cartography and ethnographies; and through their ethnographies, even where caste was not previously entrenched or enforced in India, it came to be so.

We surfaced out of that extended period and we went through the twentieth century carrying all the pain of that rule in a highly fragmented manner, so much that in most fields of knowledge we fragmented ourselves. We said this is literature but that is folk literature and folklore. This is fine and this is written but that is oral; this is good but that is Dalit literature. This is mainstream writing and that is Adivasi writing. Till this day we have not been able to describe the form of art for which Maharashtra deserves a thousand salutes—and that is the *Wari* to Pandharpur. Can there be any better form of art where millions come together, singing, dancing, losing themselves? We do not have even one word by way of aesthetic register, terminology, concept, to talk about the *Wari*. There are so many about *sajja*s, about the *gali*s in my Gujarat, but we don't have conceptual categories to describe the *rangolis*. We have trashed a huge amount of art that we express because we have fragmented ourselves in the fields of knowledge. We have created knowledges that do not relate to each other. This is documentary cinema, that is feature film; this is Bengali cinema, that is Marathi cinema, so you have different awards for them. Our institutions have emphasised that fragmentation and therefore what we should appreciate as diversity comes to us as a huge heap of broken pieces, one not connected with the other at all.

For our time, if Aristotle was thinking of unity or Bharatamuni was thinking of unity, continuity, subjectivity, for our time diversity should be the episteme, the building block of knowledge when it comes to thinking about aesthetics. Because in our times there are many other things happening. The earth is in danger; the extinction rate of the earth has gone up in the last 50 years by 4,000 times as compared to what it was in the last cycle of destruction of the species. How much we consume and how fast we are going to finish off the earth is 4,000 times more now. We are pushing everything to extinction in some kind of final crazy dance of destruction. In our time we know that everything depends on everything else. Everything is inter-connected. Poverty alone is not poetry nor is wealth. In Hampi of the fifteenth century or Jaipur of the seventeenth century wealth could be art, lavish style could be art, in the writings of Chekhov or Premchand, poverty could be art or Dalit writing. Today we know they are inter-related. Nothing in India is in isolation from what happens in Burma or Pakistan or China or America or Europe.

There's no social class that can afford to remain self-engrossed. We need respect for diversity for the simple reason that the earth will continue, will remain alive. And all of us have to accept that we belong to the earth, the earth does not belong to us. With that reverence for Mother Earth and with that reverence for diversity, we'll have to look at our arts and accept all arts as Art. That shall be our aesthetics in the future and that shall be the aesthetic in every form of expression. That is the closing sentence of Dr. Ranade's book *Indology and Ethnomusicology: Contours of the Indo-British Relationship* and it closes on this thought that regardless of whatever has happened to us, if we have to move ahead we must respect diversity. With my *salaam* to that diversity and my salute to this stalwart who introduced that thought, I conclude what I had to say. Thank you.

CONVERSATIONS

5 Language, Culture, Tribal Struggles and Indian Democracy

Excerpts from a Conversation with **Dilip D'Souza, Gulan Kripalani** and **S. Parasuraman** at 'PeaceTalks'*

DD: **Welcome to PeaceTalks from Citizens for Peace. PeaceTalks is an attempt made by Citizens for Peace to provide a forum to discuss sensitive issues in a spirit of dialogue, in a spirit of peace you can say. We also search during these PeaceTalks for ways forward for both us and for our country. Today we have with us Dr. Ganesh Devy and Dr. S. Parasuraman. Dr. Devy is the founder and the Director of the Tribal Academy of Gujarat and he has been very concerned for a long time with tribal issues and particularly languages, and Dr. Parasuraman is the Director of Tata Institute of Social Sciences.**

---

* Author's note: 'PeaceTalks' is part of an initiative by Citizens for Peace, a non-political volunteer group based in Mumbai that was formed in response to the violence that ravaged Mumbai in 1992–93. Excerpts from (the transcript of) the talk organised on 21 January 2011 are edited and reproduced here, with the kind permission of Gulan Kripalani of Citizens for Peace.

Dr. Devy, among others, has pointed out that languages really don't die in a sense, but that they are killed off; and to illustrate this our census in 1961 listed over 1,600 mother tongues in this country of ours, but in 1971 we decided to count only the languages that more than 10,000 people spoke, and that resulted in only a 108 mother tongues being listed. So what happens to the speakers of the other 1,501 languages, which are effectively derecognised by the State in a sense? Are they effectively silenced in our Indian democracy? Does democracy really exist if you're not able to tolerate this kind of diversity, if it kills diversity? Are there questions that we must raise, if there are any, about the connection between this and the rise of the whole Maoist movement? So these are some of the questions I hope we can touch on today, and I'd like to invite Dr. Devy to speak to us.

GND: The flow of time cannot be stopped. We have heard it said that one cannot stand in the same river twice, the water keeps flowing. This is true with languages as well. Languages change every day. If an expression like 'cool coffin' meant for Milton 'the watery grave', today 'cool' means for a young person a lovely cosy something.

Languages change every day. Languages change because languages are a repository of culture, and by culture of course we don't mean just *those* monuments, *those* practices, *those* systems and structures; we also have a complex set of conceptual categories that constitute culture. That is why *kaal* and *samay* do not mean the same, and neither of these mean the same as 'time' in English.

Culture keeps changing. The recognition of these conceptual categories is held together by language, and the cohesiveness of that memory makes a community a community. Languages change. They change naturally, but languages are not natural, they are a cultural product. They are not natural like the rivers and mountains.

It takes a long time for human beings to make words and to make sentences out of those words. It takes a pretty long time for human beings not just to talk about the present but also to talk about the past. Many other animal species can talk about the present. A dog can bark and say 'Some guest has come' or 'I am hungry'; but a dog can never say 'Once upon a time there was a king'. To tell a lie, to talk about the past and, as a kind of mirror reflection, about the future is peculiarly human. To be human is to have language. Language is the most distinctive mark for the human species. Without language one is only an animal and not a human.

It is said that at the beginning of the nineteenth century there were about 8,000 languages in the world. In the middle of the twentieth century there were 6,000 languages in the world, and about 2,000 languages had gone under without a trace. At present we have only 4,000 languages with us and the estimate is that by the end of the twenty-first century we would have no more than 2,000 languages surviving in condition of cultural fitness. This is a huge genocidal, maybe I'll call it phonocidal, future facing us.

All this is happening not just because the greed of many is driving the market force, trying to homogenise, bringing culture to a condition of facelessness. That, of course, is happening as the most crucial contextual factor. The corporate agenda is no doubt the agenda of imposing aphasia on all of us. But in countries like India, Indonesia, Papua New Guinea and Nigeria—the four countries with the maximum number of languages

(Papua New Guinea has about 1,100, Indonesia has 600, and according to the United Nations Educational, Scientific and Cultural Organization (UNESCO), India has only 500 languages)—a homogeneity in culture is being encouraged as a positive change. Let me explain how our country is aiding the genocidal (or phonocidal) crisis in which we are caught.

At the beginning of the nineteenth century some Indian languages were put to print. Marathi had come into print during the last quarter of the eighteenth century. In 1802 the colonial government's printing press was established at St. Fort Williams to print Indian languages, leading to the creation of printed texts. As a result, everything that was written came to be counted, but everything that was not written came to be seen as folk, some kind of 'non-truth', or merely tradition.

Scientifically speaking there is no logical link between a script and a language. Almost any script can be used for representing any language in the world fairly effectively. There are many languages that were written in different scripts at various points of their evolution. Sanskrit is a good example of this; it was written in several different scripts such as Sharda, Devanagari, in different epochs, and in Malayalam and Kannada in those regions. A language like Kannada or Konkani is being written in different scripts in various parts of the western coast in our own time. Many mighty languages do not have their own scripts. The English language, for instance, doesn't have a script of its own. It continues to use the Roman script. Nobody ever invented an English script, not because there was poverty of imagination.

During the early years of the nineteenth century, scripts became the basis of 'authenticity' and, therefore, everything that was non-scripted came to be culturally trashed. The languages of the tribal and nomadic communities came to be seen as mere mumbo-jumbo, mere baggage of nonsense, verbal concepts, non-philosophical, non-substantive burdens of the past. After Independence, only the languages that had scripts and printed literature in them were given states for themselves as in India most states were carved out on the basis of linguistic identity. And a list of 14 languages was added to the Constitution as a schedule: the Schedule of Languages. Today, the Eighth Schedule has 22 languages included in it. Whatever funds the government spends can be spent only on schools and colleges in those languages. This means for languages other than those 22, no government funding is available; and if funding is not available, children have to study through some other language. For them, when they grow, livelihood becomes available in some other language. As a result, one's mother tongue becomes a liability.

The State has aided the decline of these languages quite systematically. As Dilip mentioned a while ago, after 1972, Bangladesh was created on the issue of language, and therefore the 1971 census data, which was released for the public towards the end of that decade, did not publish the statistics related to languages spoken by less than 10,000 people. I gather now that in the coming years, the Government of India has a plan of releasing data related to only the languages spoken by more than 25,000 people. If this happens, the figure of 108 will further go down to 40 or so.

I think we are systematically killing the non-Scheduled languages. If you look at the surface of the earth, you'll notice that at the beginning of the twentieth century every 4,300 square miles had one language. Today, every 40,000 square miles has a language on average. And in future, 4 million square miles may be left with only one language. God forbid, but if we come to such a pass, the valuable knowledge that these languages hold, the wisdom of centuries about ecology and all else that the languages contain will be gone.

In the Parliament of India only 4 per cent of all Indian languages were ever heard in the last 60 years. If every language is a unique worldview, then approximately 1,600 of the existing worldviews in India were never heard in the Parliament. It is probably because of this that a strange kind of alienation has emerged between the political class, to whichever persuasion it belongs, and the people who speak those languages. That is not a good omen for a large democracy. In such a situation—as history shows again and again—societies take to violence. When cultural identities are coercively taken away and communities are punished with aphasia, they retaliate. The example of the Roman Empire is well known; the people called 'barbaric' or 'those who spoke the vernaculars' caused the destruction of the empire. I am afraid if the situation persists, an increasingly violent society will be born. The people's violence then will be countered by the violence of the State, which is faceless and far worse and far more cruel, more inhuman than the violence born out of a sentimentality about the loss of culture. I think we are heading in that direction. If we wish to preserve peace and if we learn to be tolerant—which is the hallmark of a democracy—we will have to look at the question of speech again and remove the tyranny of State and scripts, and learn to respect speech and language. India must do it because it is one country in the world which has a continuous history of spoken languages. And if *we* do not value it, learn to respect it, who else will? Certainly not those who are rooting for the idea of a city which is a place of malls and halls.

DD: You mentioned the corporate agenda to homogenise us, and to impose what you call aphasia. Can you tell us, why is that the corporate agenda? How does it benefit the corporations of the world to do that to us, or to all these languages that disappear?

GND: I have no doubt that you have read George Orwell's *1984*. In it, a new language is invented because a language is the people's memory of concepts and categories. In Communist Russia, there had been that language fanaticism of the State. In China, with a population larger than India's, languages have been destroyed, scripts have been destroyed. Control of language is another name for gaining control of the minds. If there is no language, we just do not relate to the external world, the phenomenal world. The only means of negotiation between the human consciousness and the world is language. If the rulers control language, they control the people. So if you could control language you could tell people that the best drink in the world is Coca Cola, not coconut water, or *lassi*, or *kadhi*. There are 680 ways in which India cooks potato, but then if you have a measured potato chip, of the length of say four inches and so and so width, it is easier to sell that kind of potato chip.

It's not me but Gandhi who said that the basis of the industrial civilisation is greed. Gandhi had opposed the idea of that kind of civilisation in his *Hind Swaraj*. The profit-driven corporate agenda is in favour of a greed-driven business enterprise and use of the intellect, both human intellect and artificial intelligence. Diversity is seen as a challenge to that goal of homogenisation. People who have preserved diversity are people who respect a need-based life; they know how to do with the minimum. I know that not long ago the people in this country could drink water anywhere, whether it was potable or not, but today we have to drink only bottled water. The airlines do not provide drinking water; but not getting free drinking water and getting the bottle is seen as 'development'. The entire infrastructure that is being built around us today requires land. A lot of land has gone for creating the infrastructure. That land belonged to people who had been preserving diversity.

Let me go back to what Dr. Parasuraman said—a very valuable observation on the situation of the tribals—the creation of forests in this country. Here one is not talking of *trees*. If you open the *Oxford English Dictionary*, you get two prominent meanings for 'forest'. The first meaning is 'a bunch of trees'; the second meaning is 'the land in possession of the forest department'. The British created their forest department here in India. They did not create a mechanism of regularly and adequately planting trees. Rather, the forest department was an institutional mechanism for chopping trees.

The Germans created a forest department in Germany in order to build their navy, and they planted trees there. That's why you see all those German trees with the same height, same width, same girth! The British created their forest department in India because Britain didn't have land mass. Approximately two-thirds of the land in India in the 1860s was brought under control of the Forest Department, which worked under a law bringing in the notion of the Sovereign Domain. Every community living in those areas was listed as a tribal community. That is where the problem started. The nature of ownership given to the tribals in those areas was such that they could technically own the land but were not allowed to transfer the ownership. The ownership became non-transferable, although inheritable. In one sense, the tribals were never fully given the ownership of their own land.

In Washington, the Gallery of Indigenous Peoples is returning the artefacts to the community; but in India the forest land was not returned to the tribal people. The British created India and Pakistan at the end of their rule, but in one sense they created two nations—I'm sorry these are strong words—within India at the beginning of their rule by creating forest land and revenue land as legally valid categories. I think the corporate agenda is not something of the year 2010 or 2000 or 1991 when India decided to go liberal. The idea begins in a machine-driven idea of civilisation where the dignity of humans and the human sentiment began to lose value.

GK: **If language's primary function is to communicate, then—and I genuinely want to know—isn't it better to have one common language? How do I communicate with thousands of tribal people? I have no language to communicate with them, nor do they have any to communicate. So how do we resolve this? I mean on one hand we do want diversity, and on the other we do want a way of common language.**

GND: The Latin term *communicatus* has its root in the term 'community'. Without communication there is no community at all. What a community does is to communicate; to be a community is to communicate. Suppose, for example, I am under pressure to learn five languages in order to communicate with people who will learn only two, will that be a fair deal? Obviously it won't be, particularly when I have fewer means to learn these languages. In our country we adopted a three-language formula for schools, and it was interpreted in a rigid way, which is: 1) the state language, 2) Hindi and 3) English. Suppose we allowed this three-language formula enabling whoever wanted to study *any* three of the hundreds of Indian languages and appear for the Board examination, the heavens aren't going to fall. But that will surely allow tribal children to study in their own languages up to the 10th or the 12th standard. This is an argument we have taken up with the Human Resource Ministry: to allow that three-language formula in a realistic way, rather than punishing those people for not having scripts at the colonial time.

GK: **Now we have the internet which has a language of its own, and it is unstoppable. Perhaps it has done a lot to bring together all kinds of people, and also apart, but it is here and I don't think it is going away anytime soon. So what is the future? Is it ideal to have the whole world speak one common language, so that some people don't have control over knowledge, and then of course have lots of their own individual languages flourishing? What is the future?**

GND: The question you raised is a very important one and it gets raised again and again. Pegasus is seen as a symbol of imagination without reason. Equus is a horse which has a sense of going ahead without any memory of what was left behind. We have of course the *ashwamedha yagna,* but in [Girish Karnad's play] *Hayavadana* you have a half-horse and a half-human, waiting to be fully human again. However in the end it is not fully human but fully animal. In the wonderful and fascinating world of cyberspace, Kubernetis or Cibernetis was a sailor who could keep his ship steady amidst tossing waves. Coleridge's father had such a painting in his house. The entire sea is violent in the painting, but there is a ship steady amid the tossing waves. He wrote those lines about a ship standing still in the middle of a storm. I think in the wonderful world of cyberspace we will have mastered the command, the ability to communicate with everybody in the world with hundreds of languages and be confined physically to a real place which is filled with silence and no possibility of language. And this is not the future; this is the present staring us in the face. Now we are not following Pegasus, Equus or *Hayavadana*, but we are following an artificial intelligence, hoping that it will solve many of the problems that human intelligence has created. Perhaps all of us will become artificial intelligence and have no human language, but have a wonderful ability to communicate with the rest of the world in the stunning silence of lonely rooms. Such a silence cannot be understood as peace. Peace is silence with life in it, with possibilities within it.

6 Multilingualism and Cultural Pluralism

An Interview by **Chitra Padmanabhan***

CP: What was the aim of the People's Linguistic Survey of India?

GND: I have always felt that Indians relate to languages very differently from people elsewhere in the world, so I wanted to know how communities across India perceive their languages. Primarily we wanted to find out how many living languages India has. We also wanted to see if language could be made into a fulcrum of micro-planning for development in diverse ecological and cultural contexts, especially among fragile coastal, island, forest and hill communities.

Working with tribals on their languages at Bhasha since 1996 helped me realise that there was no need to unduly privilege scripts—even English does not have a

---

* Author's note: This interview, conducted on 27 August 2013 in Delhi, was first published as 'We are talking more using fewer words', in *The Hindu* on 3 September 2013, and is reproduced here with the kind permission of Chitra Padmanabhan and *The Hindu*.

unique script of its own. Hence the thought that most other languages are derivative forms of Scheduled languages disappeared from my mind. I started according smaller languages greater respect.

CP: **You looked towards communities to conduct this survey as well.**

GND: This kind of survey needed to be done by the communities themselves. Also, when you have no money, only people can be with you! Bhasha built upon and extended its networks in states, trained and mobilised about 3,500 volunteers—academics, language experts, authors, school teachers, farmers, activists, bus drivers, and nomads. They worked with their linguistic communities in their respective states. An 80-member editorial collective joined us later to ground the project academically. This was not a door-to-door census, nor a marketing survey. Importantly, the respondents' degree of intimacy with their respective languages was 100 per cent.

CP: **How was a language identified?**

GND: Over the years we have arrived at a simple format. For non-Schedule languages, each community produced a 20–25-page essay: what language name, language history and peculiar features does a community recognise? What is its grammar? To avoid the risk of a stray concoction, the community must provide folk songs, stories or written literature as language evidence.

The format also included kinship terms, for we are a society of relationships, and terms related to time (memory) and space (imagination), which acquaint us with a community's unique worldview, as do terms for colours and specific geographic features (snow in mountainous areas, water and waves in coastal areas).

Scheduled language formats had more domains—cinema, music, media, technology, education, governance—and was more extensive. Sometimes, formats were adapted for special needs.

CP: **It seems to have added up to a monumental effort.**

GND: In four years we have documented 780 languages. There are 22 Scheduled languages, 480 tribal and nomadic languages, 80 coastal languages, major regional languages not yet in the 8th Schedule (Tulu, Kutchhi, Mewati), and international languages spoken in India. The survey will be published in 50 volumes by Orient Blackswan[1]... There are state-specific volumes and volumes with national overviews on themes like Scheduled, tribal, and coastal languages; Indian languages in the diaspora and international languages in India; and, kinship, time and space, among others.

This is India's first baseline survey through a quick, non-hierarchical, public consultation and appraisal. Unlike George Grierson's focus on language genealogies in his pre-Independence *Linguistic Survey of India*, our focus was on language groups in each state to know their perceptions about their languages. Acknowledging the self-respect of all, especially fragile speech communities, as enshrined in the Constitution, was an important objective.

CP: **How many of these languages are endangered?**

GND: Officially India does not acknowledge endangered languages. The 1961 Census recorded 1,652 languages. Since the 1971 Census—following the Bangladesh war when East Pakistan cited language as a reason to break away from West Pakistan—languages spoken by less than 10,000 people have been lumped as 'others'. We deserve to know how many languages our country has.

CP: **What does the survey indicate about the state of Indian society?**

GND: Kinship terms are shrinking in most languages—'mummy' has replaced *amma*, and papa, *bapu*. Terms for distant relations are losing ground, reflecting kinship erosion. Weakening ecological bonds are reflected in people's inability to name surrounding trees or birds. Terms for forms of prayer are also shrinking. Interestingly, while migrations are encouraging a growing multilingualism, we are talking more using fewer words.

CP: **How fragile are India's tribal speech communities?**

GND: In Jharkhand, where Hindi is understood by all, 16 major tribal languages are thriving. Across Rajasthan, Maharashtra, Gujarat and Madhya Pradesh, Bhili language varieties are in ascendance, a pointer to the Bhils' economic betterment and greater self-confidence about their language not being useless. Unlike Santhals, Mundas and Gonds, Bhils have not experienced Naxal activity. Due to some links to land-related activity, tribal languages seem reasonably intact.

CP: **Have any communities suffered a dramatic loss of language?**

GND: For coastal communities, hit adversely by changing sea farming technology, a wonderfully abundant terminology for fish and waves is of no use in inland areas. Similarly, nomadic people, formerly stigmatised as criminal tribes, try to conceal their language to get away from their stigmatised identity.

CP: **Is there a link between a state's development and its language status?**

GND: Prosperous Haryana has very little linguistic diversity, unlike developed Maharashtra [which has nearly

50 languages] and Karnataka [which has nearly 20 languages]. Language diversity survives only in states with more inclusive prosperity. Encouraging inclusive development is one way of averting the extinction of linguistic, cultural and biological diversity, nurtured over centuries by speech communities.

If Planning Commission data—the Rural Development Ministry probably has the most reliable data about people in India—were combined with the PLSI, effective micro-level planning for economic growth and language conservation would be possible. Local languages can be used for education and healthcare. Local growth can be a global developmental principle, not the other way round.

CP: Why has language never been seen as a fulcrum of development?

GND: A 200-year-old predominance of printing gives languages with written literature more importance. Only those languages entered the 8th Schedule, [and] got state recognition. Decision makers, too, emerged from these languages. If every language is a unique worldview then statistically not more than four per cent of Indian worldviews have been articulated in Parliament. We need to reverse this colonial amnesia.

CP: What next?

GND: We have begun a people's ethnographic survey of India to compile 800 monographs in three years. Let communities tell us who they are and their ideas of enmity, friendship, suffering and joy. On September 7 [2013], in an event planned with the Sahitya, Lalit Kala and Sangeet Natak Akademies, we will launch a people's eco-cultural survey of India. Let the culturally cohesive communities articulate their deep-rooted affinities to ecological, linguistic and culture areas extending beyond administrative districts. The three surveys can help build bridges among diverse language communities, strengthen Indian multilingualism and cultural pluralism, as well as the process of building India as a composite linguistic and culture area.

Many well-intentioned initiatives flounder as we don't know what India really is. In my small way I'm trying to bridge the divide between thought and life created by colonialism. This method will have mistakes, but I have faith in my mission and the hope that future generations will improve on my work.

Notes

[1] So far, 25 volumes in English have been published under the PLSI series.

7 More Intuitive, Less Rational

An Interview by **Kiran Singh***

KS: Bhasha is an idea, an institution, and now, a movement? How was Bhasha conceived and launched?

GND: In my first book, *After Amnesia*, I had to deal with 'major Indian languages'. In those days, they were described by the term 'vernaculars' or as 'regional languages'. I did not think either of these descriptive labels was good enough. Besides, it was cumbersome to use in every instance the longer label 'the modern Indian languages'. Therefore, I decided to offer a one-line explanation at the beginning of my book and describe all of these languages as '*bhasha*' or '*bhashas*'. It was simpler. After the book was published, I noticed that several critics liked the convenience of the term. Prof. U. R. Ananthamurthy and Prof. Meenakshi Mukherjee accepted it, and put it to use in their writings and lectures. Soon, the term acquired currency in English. Hence, when I decided to move to work with

---

* Author's note: This, as yet unpublished, interview was conducted on 25 November 2014 for the proposed e-journal *Bhashapatra*, and is reproduced here with the kind permission of Kiran Singh.

the languages of the Adivasis and nomads in India, I thought it would probably be better to keep the same term in use rather than locating another. Thus, the research centre that I set up was called 'Bhasha'. Often, friends and visitors asked me if it was an acronym, and I had to explain that 'Bhasha' is simply 'the language, the voice, the definition.' I decided there shall be no standalone logo for 're'presenting Bhasha. Thus, the word became the logo.

The activities in Bhasha were never conceived as 'pure' research. I have always found the idea of a group of thinkers who do nothing but just think somewhat comical. I wanted these thinkers to work, to act, to be part of the people's life. In fact, I decided to go to the opposite extreme and to get together a group of those who knew only how to work, to act, and to them, bring home the beauty of philosophy. In the process, I had many surprises to encounter. I soon learnt that these people already had a great innate sense of philosophy. It was just that no one had the time to spare for listening to them. So, I decided to 'listen' to those whose voices have been silenced by various processes of history and by those who have monopolised 'speaking'. Thus, gradually Bhasha Research Centre became a platform for the voices of the unheard. Since the numbers of such groups in the country are very large, their coming together gave Bhasha the character of a movement.

KS: How was this initiative backed by your family and friends?

GND: The 'initiative' was not in the nature of an enterprise or initiative. It was a natural process which unfolded step by small step, imperceptibly, unobtrusively, and in a very pleasing way. There were no violent debates and discussions before any big and dramatic decisions were made, for the decisions involved were neither big nor dramatic. Imagine if you decide to speak the 'truth' or follow 'non-violence', would there be any visible disturbance in your normal life? I guess, none very much. Something of that kind happened when I decided that I shall spend time listening to those whose voices have been suppressed. I had no plans of taking up this mission as a political activity or as an intellectual project. It was a simple change in the way I and my family led our daily lives. Thus, there was no drama or theatricality attached to the creation of the Bhasha Research Centre. It sprang up and bloomed as naturally as the wayside cactus grows, silently.

As for the material requirements were concerned, my wife—a university professor—readily agreed to allow her husband to be economically non-productive. That arrangement worked till, after Bhasha had gained stability, I took up gainful employment once again as an additional activity.

KS: What is Bhasha's vision regarding Indian languages?

GND: One, all languages, irrespective of the number of speakers, or histories, or literary production, or social standing, ALL must be safeguarded. And whatever Bhasha can do to achieve this must be done without waiting for project funds and official permissions. For the Bhasha Centre, the Indian bhashas are a matter of a mission and not a project or a theme or activity.

KS: Bhasha is about tribal community, orality, languages and culture. But it also works with deprived, dispossessed and exploited communities, holistically leading to various initiatives. What were some of these initiatives?

GND: It was simple and easy for me to grasp from the very beginning of the Bhasha Centre that a language survives and thrives if people who speak it survive and thrive. Therefore, I saw no contradiction between non-linguistic efforts and the language-based efforts. I had absolutely no problem taking up activities such as micro-finance, primary schooling, health care, agricultural promotion, collective water and seed management. During the last 20 years, I have spent most of my time and energy in such activities for the Adivasi villages in Gujarat, visiting these villages, talking to the inhabitants, getting them involved. If I go by the speedometer of my three successive cars during the last two decades, I have travelled over 400,000 kilometres in those 2,200 villages, doing such work.

But at the same time, I was clear that these villages must be encouraged to set up magazines in their own languages, produce plays, restore the tradition of cultural fairs (*melas*). Their songs had to be encouraged. Their stories had to be heard. So I decided to create a large number of 'bare-foot' folklorists and linguists, village historians and rustic teachers, self-made actors and untutored museum curators. This, too, I did with an equal degree of passion.

The two activities, one related to sustaining life, and the other relating to promoting the expression of life, had to go hand-in-hand. Fortunately, these activities were not capital-intensive. Most of them could be carried out without having to depend on external funding. All that it required on my part was abundant empathy, unending patience and a willingness to give up my utterly spoilt literary ways of the mind. This last was the most difficult to do, but the most liberating of all. Soon after I left the

Baroda University—I was 45 by then—I inculcated in myself the desire to be free of the non-spoken word. Initially, I felt I was losing on the latest developments in my field of research. But gradually, I noticed that what I was gaining far outweighed what I was losing. In about 30 months after I left teaching, I was able to pass days without remorse if I did not read a book. This changed my life completely, and I started feeling closer to becoming human, a feeling that I had lost somewhere along the way to school in my early childhood. This new joy also gave me enormous physical energy to do many times more than what I was able to do when I used to be confined to my study desk. But more than that, my ear became sharper and my listening more perceptive.

KS: **During my visit to Bhasha's centre in Tejgad, I was impressed by the school for tribal children. Please tell us about your vision of education that has been put into practice.**

GND: The school at Tejgad did not come up as a result of any vision. There was a perceived need. I had seen Adivasis migrating for work to cities during the dry spells. This prevented them from sending their children to school. For a while, I tried to run a small learning centre in Baroda itself. It worked well. Then I asked the parents of those children if they would be willing to leave the children in our care if we decided to keep them at the Adivasi Academy—90 kilometres east of Baroda. They agreed. And so the first batch of children arrived in the Academy. At that time, a few of the young Adivasis were training at the Academy for community work. I asked them to look after the children, to stay with them in the same hostel. I suggested that rather than teaching the children, they should just take care that the children remained happy. This resulted in a daily routine for the children built around the idea of singing, storytelling and playing as the main activities. Then, slowly, in their spare time, these 'on-the-spot teachers' inducted some amount of writing, counting, map-reading, computer training and such things. Thus, over a period of two or three years, through completely unplanned experimentation, we collectively evolved the 'Tejgad model of multilingual school'. Please remember that as the experiment was not planned as a 'school', it was not necessary for us to have any 'fixed medium of instruction'. So, the teachers used any language that the children spoke, and those languages became—for that time—the languages of the class. When in later years, children came from other language areas, we started using those languages. Hence, we evolved the principle that the language of the child has to become the language of the school. This is at the heart of the Tejgad school. As the teachers speak the child's home language, the child starts liking the school. Slowly, very slowly, we introduce other languages of the state to the child and finally, Hindi and English. At the end of those three years in Tejgad, every child picks up five to six languages quite well.

There is no great vision behind the Tejgad school, except that we look at education as a process that will allow the voice of the child to strengthen, not weaken. I think this can also be my comment on what went wrong with education in our country for centuries.

KS: As the Academy promotes need-based teaching, which team was behind the curriculum design and what aspects were taken care of while planning the curriculum?

GND: We have multi-grade classes. All the children sit together. They are not in Standard I or Standard II and so on. They are all together. We do not have walls to our classrooms. Every moment is a class, every place is a class. Finally, the teacher and the students are a single 'collective in learning'.

We do not use external aids for teaching. What we use are the trees and animals and birds in the area. Children do not respond to the daily roll call by saying 'Yes, Sir' or 'Yes, Madam'; they are expected to respond with bird calls and animal calls. Very simple.

In terms of academic accomplishment, we like to train children at par with the fifth or the sixth grade in a period of two to three years. This is possible. We have done this with about 20,000 children so far and have kept records of their class work and test papers.

KS: What is Bhasha's role in the preservation of the Adivasi culture and identity, their educational, medical and financial care?

GND: It will be too long a story to describe everything that Bhasha has done. But, very briefly, we have managed to free the Adivasis from their indebtedness to private moneylenders to the tune of 64 crore rupees, offered medical relief to over 2,60,000 patients, and educated over 20,000 children.

But more importantly, we have succeeded in creating literary zeal in over a hundred young Adivasis. They are all writing today in numerous languages. More than a 100 books of their work have been published by Bhasha. We have created, from time to time, sixteen periodicals and then passed them on to the younger people to manage and run them. Two museums of tribal arts were created. Both are in very good condition. One in the Himachal at Kyelang, and the other at Tejgad itself. The library at the Adivasi Academy is the country's largest resource on marginal communities and cultures. We have documented music in several states and have been working on a national-level project—like the PLSI—on community ethnography (with 800 monographs planned). Besides, we are also trying to complete our work on the Adivasi gazetteers under the title '*Lokapatra*'. When completed, they will provide detailed information on all 43 Parliamentary Constituencies reserved for Scheduled Tribes. So, many things keep happening at the Adivasi Academy. It is always active. It knows no holiday. But all of this work is a result of the collective energy. I would not like to claim credit for any of it.

KS: **How was the PLSI started?**

GND: During the Eleventh Five Year Plan, a committee was constituted by the Human Resource Development Ministry. It had to suggest ways and means for protecting the non-Scheduled languages. I was chairing that committee. We prepared a plan, and the Ministry accepted it. The scheme resulting from the recommendations was called 'Bharat Bhasha Vikas Yojana' (BBVY). Substantial funds were allocated by the body then called the Planning Commission. Two years later, I learnt that the government had not been able to implement the BBVY. That made me sad. During the same Plan, the government had proposed a New Linguistic Survey of India (NLSI). Again, funds were allocated, but work on the NLSI did not progress beyond the very initial stage. In 2009, I decided it was necessary to bring together all of Bhasha's colleagues to reflect on this inertia. So, we convened the by-now-famous 'Bhasha Sangam: Languages at Ground Zero'. Representatives of 320 languages participated in it. It was on the concluding day of Bhasha Sangam that I announced Bhasha's intention of beginning a people's linguistic survey. That was the beginning of the PLSI. However, a lot of preparatory work was being done at Bhasha over the 14 years preceding the Sangam in 2010. In 2001, we had initiated a yearly assembly of likeminded scholars under the name 'Bhasha Manthan' (BM). Professor Lachman Khubchandani led the BM for several years. We had prepared initial formats for surveys during those BM meetings. The PLSI required further honing of those preparatory steps. We took the step forward and did so.

KS: How are PLSI and Bhasha related?

GND: Bhasha is, formally speaking, a trust. The PLSI is not a trust or an institution. It is a mission, an activity, a series of books, a cause-based collective of scholars and activists. The PLSI group within Bhasha reports to the trust body. The Bhasha Trust makes funds available as and when necessary for the PLSI work. It is binding on the PLSI to recover the funds that Bhasha has contributed. So the royalties from the PLSI publications are dedicated to the Bhasha Trust. I suppose the PLSI shall be able to square Bhasha's monetary contribution by 2025.

The PLSI records remain with the Bhasha office. That is the official address of the PLSI. Thus the PLSI is not an independent institution with any large office and office staff for itself. It works from the rented premises in which Bhasha has had its office for the last 20 years.

I would like to invite the readers of this interview to visit Bhasha, in Baroda, to see how a bare minimum infrastructure and a skeletal staff, too, can support a massive undertaking and help it go through to the end with unmatched success.

KS: **Please tell us about the philosophy behind PLSI and how it became a pan-India movement?**

GND: If a language never got into writing (or printing) for a variety of historical reasons, if that language is then counted merely as a 'dialect', if then that 'dialect' has reduced or lesser citizenship rights, and as a result of which the people who speak that language are pressurised to give up their speech, it is our republic that will be the loser. Out of this view, the PLSI decided to carry out a completely non-hierarchical survey of all living languages in the country and to register their existence in print.

KS: **How did so many people and communities get involved in PLSI?**

GND: If you do not ask for anything for yourself, if the people you speak to get to see that the work is in their interest, if they see that you are involved in it with your heart and soul, and not merely as an intellectual curiosity, they respond. They hold your hand, carry you forward, make sacrifices, lead the movement and rise to the occasion. This has happened in history so many times. But this cannot be planned or anticipated. It happens as an experience. I think the PLSI succeeded in touching the people's imagination entirely because it was prepared to be a failed experiment. If one tried to repeat it, it may not be possible to repeat it by following precisely the same steps in the same sequence. So often, friends have suggested to me that the PLSI could be made a 'case study' in a business school. I tend to think that it cannot be replicated exactly in the same way. Its plan was more intuitive, and less rational. It worked because selflessness was made the centre of all PLSI activities. Those who associated themselves with it and later found out that selflessness was required of them quietly dropped out when they found that to be selfless was difficult for them. The most difficult aspect of the PLSI was bringing together quality work along with the commitment of the participants. Quite often, those who can give quality and those who can give commitment do not belong to the same economic, spiritual or intellectual planes. Balancing the two was a challenge. I have grappled with it to a moderate degree of success because I work with the Adivasis and I can also speak language of the kind that has hold over quality.

KS: **What was the response of the Adivasi and other communities regarding the work of Bhasha?**

GND: Ecstasy, euphoria, thrill, delight, tears of joy, and anger arising out of the memory of being neglected and negated thus far.

KS: **How will the recognition and preservation of languages help the speakers of that language?**

GND: When a language wins recognition, the speakers of the language gain an enhanced cultural confidence in coping with other cultures, some of which can seem intimidating in their attitude. Teachers no longer feel ashamed of children speaking a non-standard language. Children are no longer made to feel ashamed for belonging to a different cultural stratum. Collective memory finds a little more space. Cultural practices get a breather. New creativity begins, first in spurts, then in outbursts. And a language that would otherwise disappear involuntarily gets space enough to follow the natural sequence of its rise and decline.

Recognition to a language is what freedom is to a country. No less; no more.

KS: **Would you please share with our readers any on-field experience that was particularly inspiring?**

GND: If there is a natural stream, pure and unpolluted, and if you ask someone which single drop of water is more refreshing, more soothing for a thirsty person, would it at all be possible to show a fixed spot in the stream? The entire experience from 1996 when Bhasha was created till today has been one single 'moment' for me.

KS: **Languages become powerful because certain languages are knowledge languages or languages for trade, employment and social opportunities. Without aligning the vernacular languages to these issues, how can the diversity of languages be preserved?**

GND: We generally see that languages with greater political power or economic control appear to be in circulation more than the languages with relatively less power in political and economic spheres.

However, if we look at the history of cultures, this impression does not last long. Would you not say that Urdu is an extremely well-developed language in terms of sensibility, nuances, metaphors and such devices that make a language rich? Did it have at any time in history a powerful political position, or an economic empire to support its growth? The answers to these polemical questions will be in the negative. What then made it such a well-developed language?

Think of Hindi, too. With which empire or major economic activity do we associate its phenomenal growth? There is no easy answer to that question. It is the same with Gujarati, Bangla, Telugu and Konkani. Languages do not grow by official patronage alone. They grow due to a variety of reasons—social, metaphysical, aesthetic, technological and even political. Therefore, I do not think it is at all necessary for the languages spoken by small groups to 'align' with any larger languages. We should not forget that every mighty language was once upon a time 'a small language'. Chaucer's English—the language of a very small island, spoken by a very small number (English speakers in Chaucer's era were probably fewer than the numbers that speak the Kurukh or Apatani in India today)—did well in not aligning with the Middle French or Latin of its day, languages that were 'mighty' by the standards of its times. The history of languages shows that mighty languages decline and minor languages grow and become mighty. In order to survive, it is useful for the mighty languages to 'align with' minor languages so that their own decline is averted for a while. Sanskrit and Latin did not do this, and therefore they declined quite rapidly between the ninth and the thirteenth century.

KS: In the present age of technology, what is the future of our languages? Do you see the emergence of a new language in the age dominated by developments in artificial language?

GND: The history of 70,000 years through which human languages have evolved from the simple and heavy-duty sets of oral signs to complex systems of significance have by now come to the threshold of a new phase in their evolution. Future languages shall be more dependent on visual images rather than sound-symbols. Perhaps, a few hundred years from now, the nature of what we call 'language' will have changed altogether. This is not to say that humans shall not be using voice or sounds. That they shall do; but the greater concentration of activity related to significance in the human brain will have moved its centre from the aural neuron circuits to imagistic neuron circuits. As and when that happens, 'the future' of our presently used languages will be more engrossed in their past. In any case, in the imagistic universe of significance concepts like 'past' and 'future' will not mean much. Those will be times when all tenses will have the tendency to collapse together.

KS: **The present generation of youth are global citizens. How should they be made conscious of their own language and other languages?**

GND: Good journalism, good literature, good radio broadcasts, good television programming, good public debates, good textbooks, good teachers in schools and colleges, good reading habits, good translations, good internet content, good education policy, good public space signage and arts, good language-based gadgets, all these and many more will be required. Fortunate is the country that pays attention to all of these. I do not know how fortunate India is.

KS: **What are the future plans for Bhasha and PLSI?**

GND: The PLSI volumes were prepared under certain historical conditions. They were not planned and produced in ideal circumstances. Therefore, they have some gaps. It is necessary to fill those gaps. It will also be necessary to monitor the changes taking place in the languages mapped by the PLSI. To do these two things, the PLSI volumes shall be 'revised and reprinted' in 2025. They shall also be further refined and re-published in 2035, 2045, 2055... and so on. Thus, it is expected to become an ongoing people's institution, not in terms of a building and infrastructure, but more as an idea.

As for Bhasha, we are planning to bring out a Hindi set of the PLSI volumes. We are engaged in preparing a hand-held digital device for tribal schools containing dictionaries of several hundred tribal languages. Also, a series of books on folklore is on the anvil.

As for myself, I would like to complete the creation of the 'Language Forest' (*Bhasha Vana*) at the Adivasi Academy. I am hoping that by the end of 2015, it will become fully functional.

After that, I would like to spend time experimenting with silence, observing long spells of *mauna* to see if I am able to understand speech through speechlessness.

KS: Last but not the least, what are you writing on these days, for the academic world expects your critical writings, too?

GND: I spend a lot of my time playing with Dastak, our Boxer dog at home. In my spare time, I raise funds for Bhasha and participate in the administrative work there. In the time that is left for me after these two activities, I handle the editing of the PLSI volumes that are in the press or about to go to press. Once in a while, I write. Hopefully, I shall write a good book some day. But that alone is not the compelling reason for my continuing to exist. In the past, I never planned and produced any book. Whatever I managed to produce just happened, as Keats would have said, as naturally as leaves come to a tree.

8 And We Come to a Standstill

A Conversation with **Yagnesh Dave***

YD: **Devy saheb, you speak Gujarati very well. How did you learn the language? The usual notion is that you are a Maharashtrian. Tell us about your family background as it is not clear whether you are a Maharashtrian or a Gujarati, or both?**

GND: Yagneshbhai, I cannot proceed without mentioning that in Gujarat there is a tradition of activist-intellectuals. The first and foremost example is that of Gandhiji, followed by Sri Aurobindo who was a professor in Baroda. Both were towering activists and intellectuals of

* Author's note: This was an interview originally conducted in Gujarati at the All India Radio (AIR) Baroda studio in May 2011 by Dr. Yagnesh Dave, who was then AIR station director. Because of the overwhelming response to it from listeners, he later transcribed and published it in two parts in the Gujarati periodical *Navneet Samarpan*, as '*Ganesh Devy Sathe Vartalap*', April 2014: 52–74 and May 2014: 46–84. It was translated from the Gujarati by Professor Rupalee Burke. The edited English translation is reproduced here, courtesy Dr. Yagnesh Dave, *Navneet Samarpan*, and Professor Rupalee Burke.

a stature who cannot be surpassed in a 1,000 years. There was also Vinoba Bhave. Ambedkar had a connection with Baroda and Gujarat. He was both an activist and a thinker. I am an extremely common individual within this matrix. I am not surprised by both these facets of my personality. I feel my upbringing must be at the root of this. My parents lived in Maharashtra and spoke Gujarati. They belonged to Gujarat. They were Gujaratis and their mother-tongue was Gujarati. From the time I was born until I was admitted to school at the age of five I grew up speaking and listening to Gujarati. But the school I attended was a Marathi school. I cannot say why but I got interested in learning languages. Thus, I started speaking and writing in Marathi. I had excellent teachers. This was in Bhor village in Pune. Later it was Sangli district, earlier known as South Satara. In Sangli I studied in Willingdon College and then I went to Shivaji University in Kolhapur. There I completed my studies up to Ph.D. I started studying English after joining college. Earlier I was interested in mathematics. I scored the highest marks in mathematics in the matriculation examinations of Maharashtra State, but could not speak one straight sentence in English. I could write with ease but found it difficult to speak. That is why I decided to study English. When I was 16 I resolved to read 200 to 300 pages in English every day. I continued to read these many pages until I was 42 years of age. I did not compromise on this resolve even on the day I got married. This is how I completed my education in English.

YD: Why did only English interest you?

GND: Because I was not good at English. I wanted to be successful in the subject in which I was weak. When I was 42, I got the Sahitya Akademi Award for my English book. It was then I felt that there was no longer the need to read English books daily, so I gave up the habit.

YD: What was the subject of your Ph.D. research?

GND: The poetry and philosophy of Sri Aurobindo. His complete works are compiled in 30 volumes. Of these, about 12 are on literature. *Life Divine* is in two parts and deals with his philosophy. It took him around 50 years to write the epic *Savitri*. He had begun to write *Savitri* while in Baroda and it was not completed until his death. It was published posthumously, two years after his death in 1952. Moreover, there is the volume entitled *The Future Poetry*. Sri Aurobindo has written many other very interesting poems such as 'Love and Death', 'Urvashi', and 'Baji-Prabhu'.

YD: How did you get interested in them?

GND: I felt that in those days (in the 1970s) only Shakespeare, Milton, Shelley were among those being taught. It occurred to me that there were many good writers in our country, too, who were writing in English, and that their contribution will not be given attention in England. If we do not do it, who else will? Sri Aurobindo's involvement in the freedom struggle was also a reason for my fascination for him. I completed my M.A. The very day that my examinations were over, I took a train to Pondicherry and returned after buying as many books by Sri Aurobindo as I could afford to. I remember that I had not enough money, so I sold my clothes at the second-hand clothes market and bought a second-class rail ticket to return to Kolhapur. It took me seven to eight days to reach Kolhapur. Shantinath Desai was my professor at that time. He was a well-known Kannada novelist. I told him, 'Sir, I wish to do my Ph.D. I cannot think of anybody other than Sri Aurobindo'. He agreed. I obtained a fellowship. I was 27 when I completed my Ph.D. I felt studies do not come to an end on obtaining a Ph.D. So I went to Leeds University in England and did my M.A. again.

YD: You went to Leeds on a fellowship to do another M.A. after completing Ph.D. in India? How did you manage to get a fellowship?

GND: It was the Rotary Foundation Fellowship. I did my M.A. on Irish literature because there is literature in English other than that written by English writers in England. It was while studying there that I discovered that many writers whom we call English writers are actually Irish. Oscar Wilde and G. B. Shaw were Irishmen. I also got to know about cultural relations between Ireland and India. Sister Nivedita was Irish. She visited Baroda in 1902 or 1903. Her name was Margaret Nobles. George Grierson, who undertook the 'Linguistic Survey of India', was a student of Trinity College in Dublin. He came to India because he did not want to stay in England. I became aware and got a very close view of such intercultural relationships. Later when I visited Italy, I got to know there were close ties between Italy and India, too, even before the advent of the British. What we call *jali,* stone filigree or latticework, has come to us from the *Piema Duire* style of Italy, which was created in Venice and crafted in Agra. Silk from Bharuch was exported (as is happening in our country now) for Caesar, and the Roman Senate had remarked, 'Your expenses are extravagant. Why should you import silk from Bharuch?' It is not as if globalisation in India started at the beginning of the twentieth century. India has had relations with other countries since ages past. Languages from Australia have travelled here. Sidis from Africa have settled in Gujarat. People from Ireland have come here and done good work. Thus, my worldview was expanded significantly during my stay in England. I was freed of limiting notions such as 'my village', 'my state'. I became a citizen of the world. Gandhiji had already spoken of keeping all doors and windows open. Roots, if they must be good, should be in thoughts, not in geographical places. Which village you belong to is not important; it is your ideology which is of importance.

YD: Your mind is your soil; thoughts may come to you from any direction.

GND: There is an incident in the *Upanishad*. A boy went to a *rishi* to study. When the rishi asked him what his name was, the boy replied 'Satyakam'. 'What is your father's name?' asked the rishi. 'I do not know,' the boy replied. Our tradition should be like that. Our citizenship must not be defined by our ancestors, our village or by the State but by thoughts and goals. I would say that we must build such a society in future where it should suffice to be a human being. We must start thinking of ourselves as citizens of such a society today itself by claiming to be a world citizen. This is why Tagore named his institution 'Vishwabharati'.

YD: How did you happen to come to Baroda?

GND: I came as a lecturer to teach English at the Maharaja Sayajirao University. I barely knew the city when I alighted at the Baroda railway station. The chief reason behind coming was that Sri Aurobindo had taught here at one point of time. Moreover, I had heard and read about the writers and painters of Baroda while in Maharashtra and England. I had heard about the Gujarati poet Ravji Patel, Gulam Mohammad Sheikh and Suresh Joshi. From the railway station I went to the University. After completing the formalities for joining duty, I went straight to Suresh Joshi. I was 30 and Sureshbhai was 60. I went to his room and said to him, 'Sureshbhai, I want to learn the Gujarati language'. I spoke to him in English. Sureshbhai was reading something that moment. He looked up and said, 'Please take a seat. Who are you? Where do you come from?' Then he said, 'I will teach you Gujarati'. That was my biggest fortune.

Sureshbhai was an eminent writer. Individuals from Gujarat hesitated to meet him. They were afraid of him. But never did I feel intimidated by Sureshbhai for he loved me almost as a son or younger brother. He would give me a book a day to read. That was when I started learning the Gujarati script. The result was that whatever I read was from Sureshbhai's perspective. He had very high literary tastes. After four months Sureshbhai told me he was retiring. The prospect of losing this wonderful opportunity made me sad. I told him, 'I will come every morning to whichever place you will be shifting'. He used to stay at the lecturer's cottage. From there he was to shift to Fatehgunj. I went to him every morning. This went on for a year. I talked to him about Marathi literature and in return for this *dakshina,* he talked to me about Gujarati literature. It was Sureshbhai who encouraged me to read in Sankrit. The University library had a good collection of Sanskrit books. The facility there was also good. Mr. Upadhyay was the librarian then. He made a room-like arrangement for me where I was free to take as many books as I liked. So from the books procured

I put aside whichever books I planned to read over the next ten years.

After about a year Sureshbhai and I thought it would be nice to discuss Kannada, Malayalam, Oriya and Assamiya literature. Sureshbhai had read a great deal of Bengali literature. He had been connected to several literary magazines. It was characteristic of him to launch a new magazine and float a new idea. He would launch a new magazine before the previous one was discontinued. It was his belief that each magazine must be discontinued in the same way that it was launched because these were not sponsored magazines or which carried colourful pictures and advertisements. These were thought-provoking little magazines. Together we started a magazine named *Setu* (Bridge).

YD: I read the issues while at Rajkot because I was acquainted with Sureshbhai.

GND: Later we decided to make *Setu* bilingual. Two issues each in English and Gujarati were brought out. Literature from all over India was translated into Gujarati for the Gujarati issue which contained Gujarati translations, not literature written in Gujarati. We translated some literature from Gujarat into English and literature from other languages into Gujarati as well as English. This went on for about five or six years. Midway in 1986 Sureshbhai passed away. A month later I left for England. That was the time when I had started writing a book in English which was published as *After Amnesia*. I won the Sahitya Akademi award for this book.

When I returned from England, Savli was in the grip of drought. There had been no rain for two or three years. I started relief work on a modest basis in Savli. For the first time I set aside my books to reach out to society.

There were numerous small villages in Savli at that time. (Today, Savli is an industrial centre near Baroda, but 30 years ago there were only small villages.) Jaydev Shukla, a Gujarati poet was based there. He and some university students came along with me. When I arrived here, Bhikhubhai Parekh was the Vice Chancellor. He entrusted me with the responsibility of running the IAS centre. My job was to teach the students English and impart administrative training. Around 100 to 150 students of the centre joined me in the relief work at Savli. We managed to raise funds through collecting old newspapers and *garba* programmes in Baroda. The money was used to buy fodder, medicines and food to be distributed in the villages of Savli taluka. I must confess that I was doing it out of charity. I lacked awareness of social work. I did not know of the complexities involved in social work. Shirishbhai Panchal and Gulam Mohammad Sheikh helped me to a great extent after Sureshbhai's death.

Setu continued to be published for two or three years before it was discontinued. I decided to stop publishing it although it was doing well. I knew it was said that every tragedy or comedy of Shakespeare is successful because he never exploited his success. Normally, people give up on their work when they are unsuccessful. Sequels must be avoided. Recently we had organised a big gathering in Baroda attended by representatives of 320 languages of the country. This was perhaps the first time in our country that there was a representation of such a large number of languages. Narayan Desai and Mahasweta Devi were chief guests. Narayanbhai delivered an excellent talk. He said to me, 'Ganesh, the one thing that you must do is not to organise a similar gathering again'. What he meant to say was that a good act done once in life must not be repeated. It is in this context that I feel no remorse over the discontinuation of *Setu*.

YD: Had you wished, you could have continued to work at the University and you would have scaled heights.

GND: Certainly, a very peaceful life, as professors are depicted to live in literature, playing tennis in the evening, going for morning walks, talking in poetic language, I could have led a similar life. My wife, too, was a professor. Both of us could have lived a comfortable life. But like I went to see Sureshbhai on my arrival at Baroda, I undertook other tasks. I began visiting villages on my Lambretta scooter along with my wife. She has always been by my side. We made frequent visits to Adivasi villages in Nasvadi, Tilakwada and Chhota Udepur and very often we thought of opening a school here. However, that did not materialise at that time. Also it was not possible. Our financial condition was not that sound. It was in the 1990s that I began to experience mental unease. The reason was that I had come across the language statistics of the first census. Normally, nobody feels uneasy or becomes concerned by such matters, except sometimes in post-dinner conversations. That is all. The fact was that 1,652 languages were listed in the 1961 Census, while the number of languages listed in the 1972 Census were a mere 109, which meant that 1,500 languages were delisted over a period of a decade. The reason for this was the formation of Bangladesh in 1972. The Census Authority of our country felt that if a greater number of languages were listed, it would endanger the unity of the country.

YD: It could also give rise to issues of regional identity.

GND: Yes, it could foreground identity, give rise to a tendency of exclusiveness. The government had laid down the condition that only those languages of which there were more than 10,000 speakers would be listed, and languages which did not have as many speakers would not find mention. Languages existed but they lost their existence, that is, they were alive in society but their names were wiped out. I was a student of literature and was trying to understand and study Marathi, English, Gujarati and Sanskrit. The University was paying me to stand before the class and say that language is the only thing that transforms animals into humans. The idea of being paid to go to class while so many languages were dying was unsettling. I had almost made up my mind in 1990–91 to resign from the University. I was supervising some students pursuing their Ph.D. at that time. I had other responsibilities. I had obtained a fellowship to write a book. I decided to complete tasks on hand and then go from village to village with a notebook in hand to document languages.

I had not imagined the social stress during my relief work in Savli. Similarly, I had no idea of the complexity involved in documentation of languages. My daughter completed 20 years in September 1996. The same day I bid adieu to the University and stepped out. It was not a project for which monetary assistance was assured. I had no support either. Nor did I have any expectations of receiving funding from any source. Taking up a job or obtaining funding was not what I had in mind.

I wrote a letter to the Sahitya Akademi that the many Adivasi languages that we have in our country are vanishing. There is very good literature in these languages. That you call yourself the Sahitya Akademi, you should be interested in publishing this literature. U. R. Ananthamurthy was the President of the Akademi then. He wrote to me in reply, 'I am interested. Will you compile the books for me?' I said, 'I will prepare 50 bi-lingual volumes'. This meant the writing in the original language and its English or Hindi translation. I started working on it. I had a file containing contacts I had made through *Setu,* these were writers and scholars from across the country. I wrote to all of them: 'Do you have knowledge of Adivasi literature or know of someone who has information about the same? Please send me any information you have'. I kept receiving their letters. I invited them to Baroda. I had no money for their hospitality but I made arrangements at the University guest house and my own house for their stay. This is how guests kept coming. Within a year's time around 700 persons had visited Baroda. All thanks to *Setu*.

YD: Nothing done goes in vain. In which other way was your experience of bringing out *Setu* helpful?

GND: The question was how was one to coordinate so much? We organised a small workshop in Saputara to work this matter out. The expense came to around 25,000 rupees. I remember the workshop was held in the last week of March. I am mentioning this because there is always scarcity of money in the last week of March which gets one worried. Monetary help and some students saw us through. Among those present for the workshop at Saputara were Jyoti Bhatt, Alaknanda Patel, Bharat Naik, Geeta Naik, Kanji Patel, Dahyabhai Vadhu and Bhagwandas Patel. Together we decided to work in the area of oral literature and tradition on a permanent basis. I thought there should be an academy-like institution to coordinate the 700–800 persons across the country and their work in this area. And that it should be located in a small village. This is how Tejgad, 90 kilometres from Baroda, was selected.

YD: Why Tejgad of all villages? Did you have contacts there?

GND: Firstly, Tejgad is situated on the border shared by Gujarat, Madhya Pradesh and Maharashtra, at the meeting point, at the *triveni sangam* of Adivasi culture. Fairs held at Kanwat and Chhota Udepur are famous. Secondly, the Koraj hill near Tejgad bears ancient rock paintings dating back 10,000 to 12,000 years ago.

YD: Like the rock paintings in Bhimbetka?

GND: Yes, similar ones. These rock paintings are an ancient heritage of Gujarat. Yet there is hardly any awareness in Gujarat about them.

YD: Even I was unaware of this.

GND: Someday if you happen to make a trip to Tejgad, do make it a point to see the rock paintings. The region is known for its lacquer pottery, its clay work, its textiles, and Pithora paintings. I was fascinated by all this. In a way, Tejgad is a confluence of arts. So I chose to go there. At first a small library was started in a room with one shelf full of around 500 books which would appeal to common readers. Gradually, people began to visit the library. After about a year I told some young men that we could sit together and talk. I told them that I would merely listen and not utter a single word. And the listening process was given the name 'diploma'. Fifteen of them volunteered. They were unemployed though they had college education. They were perplexed as to who was this person who had given up his job in Baroda and come here. The fifteen friends stayed together for two years from 1998 to 2000.

I remember some incidents vividly. The method of teaching was that I would listen to them and contemplate upon their questions. We began at ten in the morning and wound up at six in the evening. A family nearby provided me tiffin service for ten rupees. My friends would stand outside the room while I was having lunch. After a while I realised that they were not having lunch. So I decided not to have lunch till the problem of hunger was tackled. I would have my lunch before leaving from home and have dinner only after returning home, even if it were as late as 2 or 3 a.m. Many a times, discussions went on much beyond the concluding hour but we pulled on without food. Thus, the foundation of knowledge that we generated there was 'hunger'. The knowledge that was founded on hunger was concretised.

What was that knowledge? Five points came to the fore. That an Adivasi village must never be developed along urban lines. That the village had its own status and that should be retained; its original personality must not be tampered with. That the village must be free from hunger and debt. Those were the times when private moneylenders charged exorbitant rates of interest ranging from 60 to 120 per cent; people did not have enough clothes and food. That the village should be free of migration. That illiteracy should not be to the extent that people could be exploited; not that everybody must be a graduate but they must possess functional literacy. Those days I would have to meet government officials. I heard them say this thing is useful to the Adivasis and this is not. An Adivasi man I met told me, 'Saheb, if the number of mahuda trees increases, we will prosper'. I felt this was the biggest philosophy for development. And I accepted it.

YD: **This, because the mahuda tree is a *kalpavriksha*. Its flowers and even its branches are of use.**

GND: Yes, it is a sacred tree. There is no need to build a compound where there is a mahuda. It grows and flourishes. It gives happiness to everybody. All kinds of happiness.

YD: **The mahuda is thought of differently in the context of prohibition in Gujarat.**

GND: It is a unique tree even in that context. In France during a conversation with a friend, I told him that the wine produced in their country was from fruits, whereas the mahuda is the only liquor produced from flowers. This is its uniqueness. This is the knowledge created by Adivasis which should be accepted and respected. Two years later I told my Adivasi companions that it was time to begin work to make the village hunger-free and debt-free. We started by setting up micro-credit societies in which people would put their savings and made arrangements for them to avail of loans from local banks six months later. We had not then heard of Mohammad Yunus of Bangladesh who was engaged in the same field. I happened to meet Mohammad Yunus saheb a year ago. I told him about our enterprise which is the Tejgad model and is designed to meet the needs of the village. It is not an emulation.

Today there are 2,200 credit societies of Adivasis with bank linkage. Their total savings amount to Rs 80 crore. The idea that was worked upon for two years in a small room has led to these many credit societies which are capable of establishing a special economic zone (SEZ) in the village. These activities made me forget that I was a professor of literature who had resigned from the University. I became an activist over a period of 15 to

20 years. Not because I had a role model before me, not because it was my aim to become one, but merely because I had gone to the Adivasi village of Tejgad with an open mind to observe and get food for thought. Today I am convinced that one who is not a good activist cannot become a good writer. Tagore was a great writer because he was an activist. So were W. B. Yeats, Premchand, Kabir, Mira, Tukaram, Narsinh and Vedvyas. Vedvyas who wrote the *Mahabharata* was an activist not as the writer of the epic but because he was engaged directly in action.

YD: **Vedvyas himself appears in the text a few times as a character. Devy saheb, as far as your work for Adivasi development is concerned, it would really help if you established links at a broader and higher level with say, some organisation or the Central government or international organisation.**

GND: Let me give you a couple of examples of such linkages. I had taken up the issue of language. That is how the Sahitya Akademi Series happened. Eighteen volumes were brought out. The magazine *Dhol* was brought out. The number of Bhili speakers in Gujarat went up by 90 per cent in the 2001 census. This meant that as against 50 lakh people who claimed to be speakers of the Bhili language earlier, there were now 95 lakh people who claimed to be speakers of Bhili, amounting to an increase of 90 per cent. The people who were hitherto shy of saying they speak Bhili are no longer hesitant about it. They are proud of their language. Although it does not have its own script, it is not as if it is bereft of knowledge. It may not have a script, but it possesses knowledge. Once these statistics were released, the HRD Ministry of the Central government invited me and entrusted me with the task of preparing a scheme for endangered languages in the country. I prepared a report which was accepted by the Planning Commission and the HRD Ministry and based on that they floated a scheme called Bharat Vikas Yojana. Whether the scheme has been implemented or not, how effective it is, is a different question but the point to be made is that the beginning we had made in Tejgad had made it to the policy level.

The other example is of 1998 when we established the Akhil Bharatiya Vimukt Samaj Sangathan (All India Nomadic Communities Association). At first, creative writers came together. Lakshman Gaekwad from Maharashtra and Mahasweta Devi from West Bengal were there. I was there; then Bhupen Khakkar joined followed by Govind Nihalani and Jaya Bachchan and many others. The issues of the denotified and nomadic tribes are different from those of Adivasis. These people have been victims of great injustice. They are persecuted by the police. They are stigmatised. They live a scourged life from the time they are born until their death and even after their death because they are not allowed to have their cremation ground in their villages. We approached the Home Ministry and the Human Rights body. I remember having met V. P. Singh, Chandrashekhar, Atal Bihari Vajpayee, and Dr. Manmohan Singh. I met each one of them and acquainted them with the condition of these communities and told them that only the government could prevent the atrocities faced by these people because the law had given rise to the atrocities and only through the law could they be stopped. The oppressive 1871 Criminal Tribes Act had been thrust upon them unjustly. The Antrolikar Committee set up in

1939 consisted of Ravishankar Maharaj and Antrolikar. They travelled all over Gujarat and Maharashtra where the camps and prison-like settlements of these communities were located for undertaking a deep study. The Antrolikar Committee was indeed a good one; the Mumbai government accepted its report.

After Independence the Central government formed the Iyengar Committee on the basis of this report and which in turn prepared a national-level report and annulled the 1871 Act leading to the denotification of tribes which were hitherto categorised as notified. From 1952 when these tribes were denotified until almost the end of the century, nothing has been done for them. There has been no change in people's social attitude towards these communities. This is why these people continue to be victims of injustice and intolerance almost on a daily basis. When a theft takes place in Delhi, newspapers report the very next day that it is believed that a Pardhi from the neighbourhood is behind the theft. This is very wrong. When other crimes take place we do not associate it with any community saying the Patil or Reddy or Mehta community is responsible but communities such as Pardhi, Sansi, Chhara are immediately mentioned. This is entirely wrongful. And therefore a common Chhara child, even though he is promising, finds it difficult to study in a school or college.

A Pardhi woman had attended a gathering organised by us. She was a good singer. This was in 1998. She had come from Mumbai. We had sent her the ticket and some money. She was wearing a new sari that she had bought for the occasion. The Mumbai police took away her sari and asked her, 'From where did you get this sari?' We read of Draupadi's *vastraharan* in the

Mahabharata. It happens in our times also. The DNTs are subjected to such oppression day after day. We have filed numerous cases against custodial deaths in court. We visited the Police Academy to mobilise awareness among the police. As a result of all this the PM formed a Technical Advisory Group, of which Shri Kanji Patel and I were among the members. We prepared a report. Once the government accepts it a new law will be passed in the coming six to eight months. After 60–70 years of the Iyengar Committee there is hope that there will be a new arrangement for these people. One cannot say whether it will be done or not but we have done the work we were supposed to do. I am not a saintly man. I believe I am not a good man. But I must say I have done my bit for the DNTs. Youth of the new generation must take this process of struggle forward. If they forget, somebody will have to undertake the task all over again.

YD: **Tell us about your work on the National Tribal Policy.**

GND: The Tribal Ministry was set up in 1999. Adivasis constitute 9 per cent of the population of our country. Gujarat has an Adivasi population of 15 per cent, Orissa has 23 per cent, and Madhya Pradesh has 21 per cent. Rarely must any other class of people have contributed to the Independence struggle as the Adivasis have. The Adivasis entered into confrontation with the British in the mid-eighteenth century. And if we view history in an unbiased manner we will notice that it is the Adivasis who have not been mentally colonised; in other words they have not been victimised by Macaulay. Those who have not been mentally colonised are free. We need to learn a lot from the Adivasis, especially at the level of contemplation.

YD: I am reminded of Levi Strauss's remark that one can wait for research in chemistry or physics or space science but if we delay research in oral traditions and indigenous knowledge, it will be lost.

GND: It is important to understand the social structure of the Adivasis. Their systems, knowledge texts, thoughts—at the root of it all is one idea: that 'I belong to the earth, the earth does not belong to me.' Other communities believe that the earth belongs to us so we can undertake mining, cutting down forests and drilling the way we like. Man has invaded the earth.

In this age of climate change and global warming the world does not have a choice other than accepting the worldview of the Adivasis. I have never once thought of the Adivasis as backward in the past two decades. On the contrary, I think of how I can reduce my backwardness by observing them. It is foolish to think that I am progressive because I speak English and they are not because they do not. This is why I said that those who are not victimised by Macaulay are mentally free. There was no specific policy for the Adivasis until the Tribal Ministry came into existence in 1999, except the one formulated by Verrier Elwin.

Elwin was a devotee of Gandhiji. This clarification is necessary because his name may imply that he was a British official or that he came here to convert us to Christianity. But that was not the case. Verrier Elwin studied in England. After completing his Ph.D. he came to Pune. He got bored in Pune and came to Sabarmati Ashram. Gandhiji suggested that he learn about the Adivasis from Thakkar Bapa. Thakkar Bapa sent Elwin to Madhya Pradesh. Elwin was free of spirit and could not adjust to Gandhiji's discipline and his principles.

Overcome by boredom he came back. Perhaps he intended to tell Gandhiji that he would not be able to sustain the work. Bapu was in Mani Bhavan in Mumbai at that time. Elwin went to see him in the evening. Gandhiji told him they would talk the next morning. Elwin was sleeping on the terrace, and at 3 a.m. in the night the police arrested Gandhiji and took him to Yeravada jail. Bapu remained in prison for a long time. Before going to jail Bapu wrote a note to Elwin asking him to continue with the work. Therefore, Elwin went to Chhattisgarh once again where he continued to work for the next 35 years. After Independence, Elwin was given honorary citizenship of our country. He was the first non-Indian to have got the honorary citizenship. He was a good writer. He wrote excellent English. Then the Sahitya Akademi was established, and Elwin was given the first award for English literature.

The policy that Elwin had framed for the Adivasis was accepted by Nehru. Elwin had named it Panchsheel; Nehru used the word for Indo-China bilateral relations. Elwin had stated in the Panchsheel that Adivasis must not be harassed and they must be allowed to live in their own way. That engineers from outside need not be sent among them. That they should be allowed to decide their own path of development.

Now this was way back in 1950–55. By 1999 many changes had taken place in the life of the Adivasis and in the country. No re-thinking was done on this policy until then. The Tribal Ministry was formed in 1999. It was then that the National Democratic Alliance (NDA) government decided to prepare a policy for the Adivasis. But that did not happen. Then the United Progressive Alliance (UPA) government came to power. They thought of framing a policy for which they decided to prepare a document. Then it occurred to them that a restrictive policy would not be a practical idea because the situation of Adivasis in each state was different. The issue at the root of the predicament is that of the land of the Adivasis which is in the hands of the forest department or the land of the forest department which is in the hands of the Adivasis. Both these matters need to be sorted out. It is in this context that the government framed the Forest Land Act.

Let me give you a brief background. The Franco-Prussian War took place in 1870 between France and Germany. Many European countries were involved in it. It is as a result of this war that the country of Germany, which was earlier Prussia, came into being. At the end of the war Germany decided to establish a forest department to facilitate the availability of timber, the unlimited use of which would help to raise a naval force. In revenge-reaction-response to this decision of Germany, England, too, decided to establish a forest department. The British did not have the land to cultivate the forests needed for building a naval force; theirs is a geographically small country. So they established their forest department in India, and handed over almost two-thirds of our land to it. This was called 'Sovereign Domain', that is, land, including rivers, over which the king or queen has exclusive right. Almost overnight, the right over most of the land of our country, which was being cultivated by lakhs of people, went to the British Queen. This was sheer cultivable land, without trees or forests.

Those who lived on this land revolted against the British. The British compiled a list of all the communities living there and legally gave them the name 'tribes'. Prior to that, we did not differentiate between tribes and non-tribes. Who was Valmiki? He was an Adivasi. He is our epic poet. There are many examples in history which point to the fact that there was no such social classification. It is the British who created this division.

Thus, the Indian government also felt it was necessary to address the issue of the land of the Adivasis before framing a development policy for them because the British had usurped the land rights of the Adivasis. When land was given to the Adivasis, their land rights were different from the land rights of the rest of the citizens of India. Different because Adivasis have a right over land surface products, not total rights. They are tenants; they can cultivate the land, bequeath it to their children but cannot sell it. It is heritable but not transferable. Normally, when a sale deed of land is prepared it is mentioned that the rights from the netherworld up to the sky are yours. But in the deeds of the Adivasis only surface rights are given. This amounts to unequal citizenship. It is to think this matter over that the government invited experts. I, too, was invited. We had five to six-hour long discussions with the Prime Minister. We had two such discussions. The draft that emerged from these discussions was sent to the Joint Committee of the Parliament. After having taken into account objections raised in the context of the draft, an Act was passed, and is still in force. Whether it is functioning effectively or not is a matter of debate.

YD: Your organisation is named 'Bhasha'. What is the significance of the name?

GND: We have continued to use the word 'vernacular' to refer to Indian languages. *Bhasha*, which means language, is an ancient word. It belongs to the age of Panini. The word 'bhasha' bears implications of identity, of voice and language. I have had a connection with Indian languages from the beginning. I began my work in this context through *Setu*. I felt that besides languages of Adivasis, I should work with other languages, too. George Grierson, an Irishman, had undertaken a survey a century ago. No survey of Indian languages has been conducted after that. Debates on languages had begun before Independence. Gandhiji had suggested the use of Hindustani and that was an extremely important matter.

Printing started in our country in the nineteenth century. Some languages had got into print earlier at the end of the eighteenth century. A printing machine was brought to Goa by chance where printing in Kannada started but was later discontinued. The printing was done in the Roman script because the printing machines supported that script. Printing in Indian languages was started at St. Fort Williams in Kolkata after types in Indian languages were created. The British government had appointed an official named Lalujilal who is credited with printing Hindi and other Indian languages for the first time.

The languages which got into print became what we call 'literature' today; the word has a connection with 'letter'. Thus, printed letters became literature. Going by this definition, the works of not only Tukaram, Kabir, Mira and Valmiki but also the Vedas cannot be called literature. Thereby arose the false notion that only those languages which have printed literature are considered languages, and all others are dialects. But that is not the case. There is very good literature in many dialects. There is a *Mahabharata* and a *Ramayana* in the dialect of the

Garasiya Bhils in our state. According to Bhagwandas Patel, there are four epics in that dialect. I do not think there are such epics in the Gujarati language. It is not to make a comparison but to decide whether the dialect of the Garasiya Bhils should be considered a language or a dialect. Whether the Mundari language of Austric origin, which has a tradition of about 7,000 to 8,000 years old, should be considered a language or a dialect. Is this merely a question or a major issue?

Linguistics, which originated in a small country like England, had not developed the ability to recognise languages of a large and diverse country such as ours. It is with the same limitation that our people looked upon our languages and therefore, the notion that only those languages which have printed literature are languages and those that do not have printed literature are dialects came to be accepted. As a result, the formation of states after Independence was done along linguistic lines: languages with printed literature were given states; languages without printed literature were not given states. For instance, it would have been very good if the Gonds or Santhals were given a state, but that was not done. This gave rise to problems of development of these people.

A proper study of the structure of languages of our country needs to be undertaken. This is what the Bhasha Centre is doing post-Grierson. There is a slight difference between a census and a survey. The census records the mother-tongue of each citizen. Grierson's survey mentions 189 languages and 544 sub-languages or dialects. In 2006 the Central government formed a committee, of which I was the chairman. On the basis of records and information available, a list of 403 languages was prepared. These languages need to be supported because for lack of support they are dying. UNESCO had prepared an Atlas of Indigenous Languages three or four years back.

YD: Are languages on the verge of extinction like plant and animal species?

GND: There is a co-relation between the decline in bio-diversity and languages because every language bears knowledge of bio-diversity. In all the dialects or languages of the Himalayas there are around 160 words for snow. The Eskimos have 30 words for snow. There are different words for snow falling from above, snow falling in muddy water. In Kinnaur language there is a specific word for the blue of the sky during snowfall. It is the dialects which contain the maximum knowledge of ecology, not subject experts. There is a direct co-relation between the erosion of that knowledge and ecology. The decline in the number of trees and bio-diversity is proportionate to the decline of languages and vice-versa. When biological diversity vanishes, only one language, one attire, one way of eating will remain in the world, whether one lives in the desert or in the Himalayas. Hence we decided to undertake a survey of all languages. The work is underway. I have been touring all the states and conducting workshops to encourage local people to provide information. It is my wish to prepare a nice catalogue of the languages of our country. We have named this project 'People's Linguistic Survey of India'. Therefore, it has to be seen from the people's, from the speakers' point of view, not the government's.

I may say that Gujarati is a great language and there is no possibility that it will die. But the economic progress that Gujarat has made in the last 150 years (not five or ten years) is because of the Gujarati diaspora in Africa, England and Australia. The method of working in Gujarat has changed over the past 150 years and people are putting their heart and soul into the work they are doing. The work culture of our state is the best in the world. Some time back Tata had said in London that the British do not work in the way Gujaratis do. Nobody attends a meeting at 5 p.m. on a Friday evening here, but back home when we call a meeting, people work till 11 p.m. Gujarati is not endangered because of the wealth we have created. Yet there is a threat before the Gujarati language. Our language domains are on the wane. Their use for speaking is decreasing. Schools imparting education in the mother-tongue are decreasing. There is no good Gujarati-medium high school. The number of young people capable of speaking one good sentence in Gujarati without using a single English word is decreasing. Therefore, Gujarati is also endangered to a certain extent.

YD: Which other organisations have you founded?

GND: I have been associated with five different organisations. The Adivasi Academy at Tejgad is managed entirely by the Adivasis. Education in subjects related to Adivasis is imparted there. A field of knowledge called anthropology is being developed there, what we call a 'Reverse Anthropology'—knowledge of the Adivasis—which runs counter to anthropology. In anthropology people look at the Adivasis. It is my wish that the Adivasis look at the world and ask it to adopt the virtues they possess and accept what they have to offer. That is the kind of education taking place there. They have a nice library there as well as a museum. A museum has also been set up in Himachal Pradesh along the lines of the 'Vacha' museum at Tejgad; it is run by the local people and is located at the highest altitude in the world. I feel blessed for this opportunity given to me by the Almighty. I have founded an organisation named 'Himlok' which is engaged in the study of Himalayan communities.

YD: Does it range from the tribes of the Himalayas up to Nagaland?

GND: The entire region from Afghanistan to Arunachal Pradesh belongs to the same geographical region. The countries came into existence much later. The Himalayas have been there from the beginning. The imagination of political borders is like small children. The Himalayas are the parents; therefore this organisation.

I am interested in drama. In my opinion any community which claims to be civilised must be interested in drama, music, visual arts and painting; only then it is civilised, otherwise not. Drama is an ancient literary genre. From the time of Bharatamuni or Aristotle. Therefore, I founded the Budhan Theatre in Ahmedabad where children and young people from the Chhara community perform plays which are quite like the plays of Badal Sircar but slightly different.

YD: Budhan is a name from West Bengal, isn't it?

GND: Budhan Sabar Khedia was a man from the Sabar community. He was born on a *Budhwar* or Wednesday, therefore he was named Budhan. He was arrested by the police on his way to the bazaar, taken into custody and beaten up. His custodial death was recorded as suicide by the police. We filed a case in the Kolkata High Court against the police. Mahasweta Devi had taken the lead. We won the case. Justice Ruma Pal, who went on to become Justice of the Supreme Court, wrote an excellent judgment which I published in a magazine named *Budhan* that we were bringing out. Some youths of the Chhara community read the judgment and put up a play. This is how Budhan Theatre was born. Two years back they put up an excellent performance of the play *Accidental Death of an Anarchist* by Dario Fo. Then they experimented with Jean Genet's play *Balcony* as to how it should be performed if in Ahmedabad. This because Genet also came from a nomadic community. He was prohibited from travelling to many a European country. Sartre helped in getting Genet released from prison, and presented him as a playwright in France. I felt the predicament of the Chharas is similar to Genet's. Now they want to experiment with *Mrichchhakatika,* which depicts a conflict between a thief in the forest and a king in the city. There is a similar conflict between the nomadic communities and our society; therefore, the play would be performed from the thief's perspective, and not the king's or the courtesan's. Bharatamuni, I believe, was an ostracised person and was in confrontation with the society of those times which considered performing plays a crime. This is why his text is called the *Pancham Veda* (Fifth Veda). I am interested in drama and in ostracised people because I believe that there should be an inclusive society in the world without barriers of race, nationality and language and where each citizen of the world has the right to live as a human being. I am doing whatever little I can do for this cause.

YD: **I had once expressed my worry before Bhayani saheb[1] regarding the death of the Gujarati language. He said it was not likely to happen in the near future. The implication was that language is in a flux and may undergo transformation. Had we clutched hard at language, the evolution of old Gujarati from Apabrahmsha,**

new Gujarati from old Gujarati, would not have taken place. But the present situation is quite different. Do you feel languages are being erased? Earlier, languages underwent transformation and in the natural course made way for other languages.

GND: Very true. Language is fluid. There are languages which are written in one script for some time and in another script in another time. Earlier, Sanskrit was written in the Sharda script, now it is written in Nagri and Modi. The Modi script was used for writing many languages. Therefore, there is no logical connection between script and language. A language which resists transformation dies. That which undergoes transformation lives. When we try to dam the flow through artificial means it gives rise to difficulties. Especially when someone tells us that since the language you speak does not have a script, does not have a written form, we will not set up schools or colleges and universities for you; then such children have no option but to progress in a language other than their own. Therefore, if we were to prepare a map of illiteracy in our country of regions with under-developed populations, it would be connected to language. Regions where such dialects or languages without a script are spoken—I do not say languages without knowledge because many languages do not have scripts but are storehouses of knowledge—have greater percentage of illiteracy. Therefore, this issue needs serious attention.

Bhayani saheb was absolutely right. Languages do not die on their own. Many ancient words are still in currency in our country, like the word '*musal*'[2] which is 4,000 years old. It is when some law or flawed policy encroaches upon languages that they are killed. Languages are immortal but they are sentenced to death.

There is a word in the Greek language 'aphasia'; it means speechlessness or lack of ability to speak. Aphasia is being imposed upon many languages in the world today. According to an estimate of the UNESCO there were approximately 7,000 languages at the beginning of the twentieth century; by the end of the twenty-first century, only 300 will have survived.

YD: Only one-tenth of the languages of India have survived as you pointed out.

GND: Yes, this extinction of languages is aphasia. Language originated with the first utterance by a human being. Right from then until now, more harm has been done to language for dialogue in the last 150 years. This is worrying. Organisations like UNESCO are striving to preserve languages, diversity and multilingualism.

YD: Will the minor languages survive despite efforts when even major languages are threatened by English?

GND: It is difficult to predict how many will survive and how many will die in times of an epidemic. Escalated efforts have to be made to lessen the loss. We must work with the faith that less harm will be done if we make efforts.

There is a belief that if a child acquires education in the mother-tongue up to class seven, it is sustained by him. Forget class seven, education at the kindergarten level is imparted in English. Who is a great Indian writer in English? I would say Mahatma Gandhi, who did his schooling in the Gujarati medium. R. K. Narayan, who studied in Tamil. I studied in Marathi. When I write in English I am not diffident in the least. People in many parts of the world read the books I have written in English, which is not in any way inferior to any other English. Education in the mother-tongue is the fundamental right of every child and it must be so.

YD: **What is the condition of 'Adivasis' at the global level? For instance, the condition of American Indians after the Europeans took over America, or the Spaniards took over Central America, or the Portuguese conquered most of South America; the condition of the Aboriginals after the British took over Australia ... How have we dealt with the problems of the Adivasis in India?**

GND: The main point is that the words 'Adivasis', 'Indigenous', 'Aborigine', 'Maoris' came into being only in those countries where colonial expansion took place. If we ask someone whether there are Adivasis in Germany or France, the answer will be: there aren't any. There would be natives there, isn't it? But it is the consequence of colonialism to annihilate them, to impose new economic systems on the people or destroy their economy. The Spaniards burnt everything. The destruction caused by the Germans, the Spanish and the French is much greater than that caused by the British. The Dutch also caused much destruction. So did the Portuguese. Almost every country of Europe did so and it is as a result of their work that the Adivasi communities emerged. This led to the notion that they are a different community. Those who were oppressed, those who had to suffer, which communities were they? They were communities which believed in collective wealth, collective responsibility, collective rights, such was their worldview. Secondly, they were intimately connected to Nature; it was an ecological commune in which there was a harmonious relationship between man, Nature and God which was beneficial to all three. Spiritual need, in the sense that there is some power which runs the world, such a need is felt by everyone and it is manifest even in Nature in the form of strength. So it is a power which is above this non-human power. This is followed by Nature. Man comes last. The Adivasis were those who maintained harmony between these three.

Later, a society which was only after money and strove for economic progress came into being. No doubt economic development took place, but we also need to think how much happiness we experience in the course of one day. Bhutan has said one nice thing: there must be a happiness index. The number of times that we laugh in a day, that we experience happiness or sing songs in a day is the barometer of our happiness. It is a happy situation in India, whether because of Hindi cinema or something else but everybody sings songs which is a good thing. Adivasis do not have television, fridge, car and radio, but come evening and they dance and frolic and sing. Those are the wonderful moments of life, I feel.

The moment the colonials arrived in America they practically decimated the natives. Criminals from Europe were sent to Australia to settle. They destroyed the natives there. India is one country along with other countries of Asia such as Pakistan, Afghanistan and Thailand where the Adivasis survived and still exist. Our government has lent good enough support to the Adivasis. (Presently it is not to the extent that it should be. The nomadic and denotified Adivasis especially need more support). Today there are 6 to 7 crore nomadic and denotified Adivasis and 9 crore Adivasis in India, a total of 14 to 15 crore population. The total population of New Zealand is 60 lakhs. The population of Adivasis in Gujarat equals the total population of New Zealand, out of which the Maoris are barely 12 per cent which is 12 lakhs. In comparison the situation in India is fairly good.

YD: **Had Dupleix won in the Mutiny and French rule been established in India, what would our condition have been? Were the British perhaps different as rulers compared with the Spaniards or the Portuguese?**

GND: When Tantya Bhil was sent to the gallows, one lakh Adivasis had gathered. But there was not a single instance of firing. Had it been the French, Spanish or German that would not have been the case. But there is another side to this history. It is a matter of joy that there are Adivasis in our country, but that also means more responsibility on our side. In America it suffices to build two or three museums. But in our country there are 8 to 9 crore Adivasis and they need to be provided with the right kind of education and health care. There are more than 360 universities in our country but there are less than 1 per cent Adivasis in the academic staff, which means Adivasis have not reached that level. And therefore, it is the responsibility of our country and society to pay more attention to them.

YD: **Did you as an activist lend support to the protest against the leasing of the Damodar Valley in Orissa? It was a situation where both the environment and Adivasi milieu would have been destroyed.**

GND: It is true that development is necessary for all of us but development does not mean only foreign investment, productivity and GNP (gross national product). If that is the case then only when all of us are destroyed can development take place. Development without destruction is desirable. Environment is essential to prevent destruction. People's happiness is as important as their welfare. Quite often there is a clash between enjoyment and consumption.

YD: Like the conflict between economy and ecology, can we, in the context of your books, view *After Amnesia* from a broader perspective, outside the context of literature? This, because there is the colonial yoke on the one hand, and the false pride as Indians possessing a grand tradition on the other.

GND: I started writing *After Amnesia* in Baroda. When it was published, debates had begun about Gujarati literary criticism and the cultural amnesia of Marathi literary criticism. Most of the feedback that I received about my book was related to politics, science, economics and history. In juxtaposition to cultural amnesia is cultural pride. Cultural pride, too, is not desirable because as Bhayani saheb said, if culture does not lend itself to change it becomes like stagnant water giving rise to stench.

Memory, which I call *smriti,* is the element which effectively binds all types of knowledge. I received good feedback when I wrote that book. But after writing it I felt only half the work has been done. What about the history after that? What are the means to understand history? Smriti is not merely reflective; it also embodies the capacity to forget. Therefore, remembering and forgetting need to be looked at together. Reactionary action to revenge will lead to severing each other's heads on a day-to-day basis. Therefore, forgetting is just as important as remembering. Discretion must go hand in hand with smriti or else smriti will turn into insanity in the absence of thought, reflection and discretion. Then I wrote about history. I wrote *Of Many Heroes* on the various principles and traditions of history that are available to us. Rajshekhar[3] said there are two types of history. One is with a single hero; I chose the second model which talks about many heroes. It is the history of diversity which is acceptable to me.

The history that gets written is not from the perspective of the ordinary people but as the rise and fall of kings as we have known it to be. It is those engaged in subaltern studies who are writing from the common people's point of view. But they consider the history of the past one or two centuries only. In my view, history is a continuous event. It ranges from the time of the evolution of mankind until the present moment. All the currents embodied in this history are what I am fascinated with.

YD: You have worked in close association with Mahasweta Devi. From the time you met her and she accepted your invitation to come here, your bond with her strengthened. Tell us about her work and your association with her.

GND: I have been fortunate that I got to meet Sureshbhai when I came to Baroda. Soon after I met Narayanbhai Desai for the first time at the Sahitya Akademi awards function. Vijay Tendulkar had got a Nehru fellowship to work on the subject of violence, and I, too, had got the Nehru fellowship to work on the same subject. This is how we became friends. I once wrote a letter to Mahasweta Devi in 1980 in connection with *Setu*. A very well-known story of hers 'Jagmohan: The Elephant' was published in Gujarati translation in *Setu*. Later we published another of her stories, 'Seed'. But I had not had the opportunity to meet her in person. I once visited Bengal soon after Budhan Sabar had died. That is when I happened to meet her. During our meeting we got to know of our common interest in issues related to the denotified and nomadic communities. She was around 70 years of age then, and I was around 50. During that very meeting we decided that we will tour across the country and meet denotified and nomadic communities and after understanding their situation we decided to acquaint the government, the judiciary and the police with their plight, to write about them and to gather people together. We travelled by third class from Surat to Jalgaon, although Mahasweta Devi was a Magsaysay and Jnanpith awardee, a world-famous personality, of advanced age and a diabetic. Sometimes when we did not get a seat we would keep standing and talking. She would talk about when she wrote her stories and the incidents from which they emerged.

We went to Amravati. The sickle cell anaemia epidemic was rampant there. The Maharashtra government had formed a committee. Doctors had announced that this was a genetic disorder and nothing much could be done about it. They decided to administer iron tablets. Mahasweta Devi went on to write a marvellous story about this titled 'Mahadu'. Mahadu is the last surviving Korku Adivasi of Amravati awaiting his death. The British had cut down the entire forest of the Korku Adivasis to procure wood for making sleepers to lay beneath the Surat–Howrah railway line. Mahadu is unsettled by the approaching train and the sound of its whistle. He can smell the railway. He feels it is the scent of his ancestors. He races to catch the train and reaches Mumbai. In Mumbai he gets to see the substance that he had never seen in his life—food grains. As he goes on eating he grows in size. He assumes a gigantic form. He eats up entire Mumbai. His is the hunger of many generations. Gradually his head touches the sky. He bends down and gulps down the whole Arabian Sea. He plucks the stars from the sky and writes the history of the world in new letters. Marvellous story! I grasped the chemistry of Mahasweta Devi's stories, that they are based on actual experiences and not imagination. Of course, her imagination is blended because of her way with words.

Mahasweta Devi did not own her house until the age of 80. She lived in a rented house. When she first came to my house, I was not sure whether she would be comfortable in my small house. But as soon as she arrived she said she would eat only dal and rice. She is a great human being. I consider myself fortunate that I got to meet her, travel with her and learn from her how to carry out social work, when to stop and so on. One noteworthy aspect of Mahasweta Devi's social work is that she does not desire to translate it into power. Almost everyone engaged in social work nurses the ambition to make it to the Rajya Sabha. But Mahasweta Devi works selflessly and devotedly. Everybody in the country looks upon her as the Mother of the country.

YD: Tell us about your hobbies such as music, painting, travelling, food, etc. What are your sources of happiness?

GND: I have travelled far and wide. I have visited very many countries except Africa and South Africa. I love visiting cities. Especially the small winding streets. I keep walking through them for hours together, watching the people on the footpaths. This is one experience that gives me immense happiness. Barcelona is one of my favourite cities. I have been there on my own. I like Antoni Gaudi's architecture because I like things which are infinite. The city of Leipzig in Germany is another favourite. In France there are cities built on the first storey. The ground is for vehicles only. Commercial and residential spaces occupy the first floor. They are fashioned after the Russian model. But my most favourite city is in our country, and that is Kolhapur. In Kolhapur there were wrestlers; buffaloes brought to the doorstep for us to get milk. The people there are rustic, agrarian.

I also like the city of Baroda very much because it offers ample scope for the arts. There are painters, musicians, litterateurs, individuals originally from Baroda such as I. G. Patel and Bhiku Parekh who have worked at the international level. I have not seen much aggression in Baroda; struggles to demean one another are not characteristic of its ethos. But it is also true that the city was better than what it is today. It would be really nice if Baroda were to return to its former self. In Sri Lanka I noticed a street named Anand Kumar Swami. But in Baroda there is no street named after Suresh Joshi or Bhupen Khakkar. This I find inappropriate. Streets here need to be named after them. Umashankar Joshi, Harivallabh Bhayani, Suresh Joshi, Bhupen Khakkar, one can mention 40 such names. There are Picasso museums in every house in which Picasso stayed, whether in Barcelona or in Paris in France. The café which Picasso visited is also indicated. This must be done in our country, too. This helps in enhancing cultural memory.

YD: There must have been times when something good that you said led to a controversy. Has this upset you?

GND: Yes, it has upset me. It may have happened that I may have hurt the sentiments of some individuals by my words or my writings. It happens sometimes. But I recall two controversies in the context of Gujarat. A book review magazine had asked me to review ten books written in Gujarati. With the help of ten persons I collected critiques in English. These were ten books

I thought were appropriate. I felt that people outside Gujarat would get to know about books from Gujarat. I had to also write an article on the then present state of Gujarati. This was way back in 1990–91. I wrote that the condition of Gujarati is worsening. Before me Suresh Joshi had said that Gujarati literature is on oxygen on the deathbed because the children of Gujarat do not read enough. The habit of reading in Gujarati is on the decline. I wrote what I felt about the situation. I received many responses saying I have put Gujarat to shame. That I would not have been able to say so were I in Maharashtra, West Bengal or Kerala. I believe that the rape of girl children by ministers in Kerala is bad; there are bad elements in Maharashtra responsible for social unrest which is bad. But it is a fact that Gujarati readers do not read Gujarati books to the extent that Malayalam readers read Malayalam books. There was a hullaballoo and many magazines carried editorials on the topic. Four or five were in my favour, 15 to 20 were against what I had written. Twenty years after this incident a big campaign was undertaken to increase the number of Gujarati readers in order to keep Gujarati language alive. That was when I felt that what I had said two decades ago was not wrong. However, I now feel I could have said the same thing in better words, but that is an ability I lack.

The second time it happened on the 1st of May. Every year I go to Dandi where Adivasi friends gather together and each one pours out his heart. This programme was started ten years ago with the blessings of Narayan Desai. Five or six years back when I returned from Dandi to Baroda, the city was under curfew. The next day I read in the newspapers that the Municipal Corporation had razed to the ground a *mazar* (tomb of a Muslim seer) and had parked a police jeep where it once was. This mazar is in the *Shukravari* (Friday flea market) area. There is a gate towards Champaner and since there is a mosque there, the flea market was held on Fridays. The mazar must have been of some seer connected to the mosque just as saints connected to temples live in the vicinity. In the nineteenth century when a complaint was filed in connection with the mazar, His Highness of Baroda had the market shifted to a new building which came to be called Khanderao Market. The office of the Municipal Corporation of Baroda is housed in the Khanderao Market building. This very corporation decided that the mazar was an obstruction and it should be razed. This led to a protest by the local people and resulted in a conflict between the police and the Muslim community of the locality, due to which the curfew was clamped.

Two or three days later while talking to a *Tehelka* reporter I said that if such incidents continue to take place in the city I will find myself isolated. Who will I be able to have a dialogue with? I feel as if I am walking in the desert. You have asked me to write a creative piece, so I wrote in metaphorical terms: 'A lonely man walking in a desert'. The reporter published it after asking me if I had no objection to it. I gave him my assent saying these are merely my thoughts and that he could publish the piece. But I feel it was written in very strong words. There was nothing wrong about my thoughts; I still stand by them. There was a controversy. No writer had written anything when riots had taken place in Gujarat before. My statements provided them with the opportunity to air their views. Some said there must be harmony in our society; others said the writing was anti-Gujarat and so on and so forth. It is the usual thing here to brand as 'anti-Gujarat' anybody who speaks the truth and thus dismiss the matter. This is not appropriate. I live in Gujarat and work for the Adivasis of Gujarat. My parents were Gujaratis. I owe a lot to Gujarat for giving me respect, for giving me an opportunity to live. I do not consider myself either as belonging to Maharashtra or Gujarat. I believe that I am a citizen of this world. This is how there was a little misunderstanding. Actually, it is always good to have a debate. If everybody was to agree to everything, society would lose its capacity to think. There must be discussions. It is up to the individual to decide which thoughts are good and which are not. Discussions will help in enhancing communication skills or discourse. That way we will learn the art of dialogue. It was my mistake to have used strong words.

YD: Ghalib has said, '*Hazaron khwaishein aisi ke har khwaish pe dum nikle*'. Is there any such *khwaish* or desire which you feel you would not mind spending all your energy to fulfil?

GND: Forty volumes of the Linguistic Survey are on the anvil, eight in the bhashas, 12 in Hindi and 20 in English. The total number of pages is approximately 30,000 pages. This will take ten years' time. It is my strong desire to write a book on the *Gita* because it has provided me with a lot of support in life, a lot of strength. And I have my own perspective on the *Gita*. I will get down to writing it when I have some respite from touring. Simultaneously I also want to write about Indian cities. Streets and houses do not make up cities. Life makes up cities, *pols* (living quarters in walled city spaces) make up cities, and lanes make up cities—cities which accommodate all strata of history. This is what I want to write about. Mine is an inter-caste marriage. My wife is from Karnataka. She is not a Muslim or Hindu or Christian but belongs to another religion. The two of us decided to get married. We submitted our Ph.D. theses the same day. She has never expected me to give her a sari or gold or silver. It is only because she has stood by me that I have been able to accomplish what I have. The cart cannot move if both wheels do not move together. It is my good fortune to have a wife who is extremely intelligent, dynamic, noble in thought and fearless. Fearless because of non-attachment. I have learnt a lot from her. She lends me strength.

YD: **Any other desire? God help you fulfil it...**

GND: I do not desire to acquire anything. I have done a lot of damage. I will accomplish my work and go away. I was around 40 years of age when I began reading the *Gita*. I felt that one must never fear death. I have never desired wealth. I am not a saint. I repeat I am a bad man. But I do not wear the robes of a saint and will never do so. I do not go to the temple often. Whatever there is, is there in the heart and mind. I have stopped taking medication since I turned forty-five. Once even when I was bitten by a snake I did not resort to medication. I do not fear death. When death comes I will accept it selflessly. I do not believe life and death are two different states. Nor do I believe that after death we inhabit another world. I believe that we will inhabit another age, an age which would have passed. Time is bound to pass. Therefore, we will but have to inhabit an age which has already passed. Our race is against time. Time is more powerful than us and there will come a moment when it will continue to run but our capacity to run will be exhausted. And we will come to a standstill.

Notes

[1] Dr. Harivallabh C. Bhayani (1917–2000) was an eminent linguist, literary critic and translator engaged in the study of medieval Gujarati.

[2] *Musal* is a pounding bat used for crushing grains and condiments, traditionally an essential household item. It was also used as a war weapon in ancient times.

[3] Rajshekhar (or Rajsekhara) was a tenth–eleventh-century Sanskrit poet, scholar and author of the treatise *Kavyamimansa*. He spoke of the *Ramayana* as an epic with a single hero and the *Mahabharata* as an epic with many heroes, treating the two as prototypes of, what he described as, 'history'.

9 Beyond Cultural Aphasia

A Conversation with **Rossella Ciocca***

The sudden outburst of anguish from so many writers and artists over the last two weeks has taken the country by complete surprise. It has occupied substantial media space and engaged the curiosity of citizens. Various political parties have commented on it by placing themselves as allies or adversaries. The Union Minister for Culture, too, has responded by way of dealing with what he thinks is 'culture'. Over the weekend various magazines and literary supplements will have devoted their precious space to this 'rather strange phenomenon', analysing the whys and hows of the eruption. A week from now, the meeting of the Sahitya Akademi Council will have already joined the ranks

* Author's note: A version of this conversation, conducted over e-mails in 2015 as part of 'Dakshinayan: The Writers' Resistance Movement', was first published as 'Beyond Cultural Aphasia: A Conversation with Ganesh Devy on Indian Adivasis', in *Anglistica AION* 19.1 (2015), 25–35. It is reproduced here, with modifications, with the kind permission of *Anglistica AION* and Professor Rossella Ciocca, University of Naples 'L'Orientale', Naples.

of events past, generating responses and counter-responses. But will the winter of Indian Writers' Discontent (IWD) be remembered a few months or a few years from now? I would like to place my observations here in the mode of a future historian of the present.

The most important element of the IWD is that it is not an organised movement or a conspiracy. One of the politicians commented that this is an engineered disaffection for the State with backing from a political party. This view has the fatal flaw in understanding the IWD as a social or a political movement. It is neither engineered nor is it planned by any political party, outfit, social organisation or funding agency.

The poet Keki N. Daruwalla made it a point to stress in his open letter (14 October 2015) to the President of the Sahitya Akademi that he is not prompted by any political ideology: 'I wish to make it clear that I have no party leanings. I was no lover of the corrupt UPA 2. People like the late [Narendra] Dhabolkar were murdered during the previous dispensation.'[1] This has been more or less the strain in all of the statements issued by writers who returned their honours.

The writers who responded to the suddenly manifest cultural impulse are not from any single political background or affiliation. The question of political affiliation does not even matter in this unique phenomenon. What matters is their emphasis on the increased intolerance in social life. In my statement sent to the Sahitya Akademi I have described them as 'writers and thinkers who have come forward to rescue sense, good-will, values, tolerance and mutual respect. Had this not been so, why would we be remembering the great saint poets who made our modern Indian languages what they are today? The great idea of India is based on a profound tolerance for diversity and difference. They far surpass everything else in importance.'

In Daruwalla's words, 'The landscape that confronts the writer today is bleak ... Faces will continue to be blackened with paint and painters like M. F. Hussein will be forced into exile. A writer like Taslima Nasreen will have to leave Kolkata under a Leftist regime. Statesmen will continue to be praised for their nationalism "despite" the fact they are Muslims. Mob murders will continue to be described as accidents.'[2]

What is at stake in this movement is much larger than a given political party, a ministry or a single institution. It is an expression of the need to re-imagine India, to humanise it, to sensitise it to the core of not just democracy but civilisation itself. At the heart of our great democracy is the idea of diversity and respect for that diversity. Respect for those who are not like oneself requires an ability to listen to different voices, a high level of tolerance. Democracy can be deepened by tolerance, and conversely it can be weakened by intolerance. Civilisation can be enriched by respect for life and other ways of looking at life. Writers today have stood up to remind the country that weakening the foundations of democracy will be at our own peril.

The phenomenon is reminiscent of the great work that the medieval saint poets did in so many *bhashas*, the thinkers and social reformers such as Namdev, Tukaram, Mira, Kabir, Surdas, Jaydev, Akka Mahadevi, Tyagaraja and so on who created the great Bhakti movement. And it is their contribution to literature and languages that shaped and nurtured our modern Indian languages since the eleventh century.

The twenty-first-century IWD should be read in terms of the Bhakti movement and not as political agitation. So pervasive is the discontent and so large the scale of its manifestation that perhaps it will one day come to be seen as a turning point in Indian literary history and one may have to speak of the pre-IWD literature and post-IWD literature. It is too soon to surmise this, but in time we will know if this is so.

Colonial/Postcolonial/Neocolonial: Historical Precedents, Post-millennial Indian Politics

RC: **The first question I'd like to discuss with you is about a possible ongoing colonial legacy on the system of inequities still suffered by Indian Adivasis. I mean, starting from the objective observation that the most part of India's eighty million Adivasis, after 68 years of Independence, still live below the poverty line, lacking education, economic support from the State and access to healthcare, do you see a sort of historical continuity in the passage from the colonial archive where tribals figured both as rebellious or even 'habitual offenders' to the postcolonial scene in which they are presented usually as 'backward' and not rarely as threatening actors in insurgent movements against national security?**

GND: Though humans are gifted with the twin power to remember as well as to forget, memory as well as amnesia, histories invariably continue to stick to our everyday existence. The way we walk, eat, exchange opinions, form thoughts, create what we call beauty—all of these carry invisible but multiple layers of history, many pasts that the mind may forget but life does not. The colonial experience in India was protracted and pervasive. It affected most aspects of how we know ourselves and how we conduct ourselves. Our idea of justice and our perception of injustice, too, were deeply affected by the colonial notions of law and order, fairness and impropriety. Besides, after Independence, it was not as if India started on a blank page. Neither the colonial process nor the experience of de-colonisation in India can really be compared—except superficially—with those processes and experience in Australia or Canada.

For civilisations that have long-standing legacies, these things work differently. In India, there already was a surplus of inequality prior to the colonial rule. The colonial rule compounded inequality by bringing in agents of change not known before. These included a notion of regulated citizenship that worked less through affection and more through economic norms. Those who could pay taxes, or had land-related occupations, were more easily acceptable to the colonial imagination of citizenship (as subject). The nomads and the Adivasis fell out of that framework and came to be seen as distant from the State.

During the post-Independence period, this distance was sought to be reduced (not entirely eliminated!) by creating a 'Schedule of Tribes' and a 'Schedule of Castes' for receiving positive discrimination. But, the mindset of the people did not change in tune with the spirit of equality enshrined in the Constitution. Besides, India's transition to a technological and industrial economic power required an unopposed access to areas in the tribal forests for mining. The scale of this operation has been really massive. A lot of displacement and disempowerment arise out of the post-Independence industrial activities. But, carrying out those activities remained easy as the Adivasi had come to be seen as 'a distant citizen' during the colonial times. One can therefore say that the alienation of Adivasis from the Indian State, and the vast inequality with which they are saddled have roots in the colonial structures, but these have seen a rapid increase in the last half-century.

In every age and every society, those who are most deprived of the economic means and access to improved life conditions come to be seen as the potentially 'dangerous' section of the society. Think of the Gypsies in Europe. The 'denotified' communities in India have faced a similar challenge. It combines social stigma with economic deprivation.

RC: **Considering your peculiar historical knowledge, is there a shared logic in the various 'Criminal Tribes Act(s)' (1871, 1921), 'Land Acquisition Act' (1894) and 'Indian Forest Act' (1927) of the colonial period and a sort of internal neocolonial present in which, however 'denotified', tribals are still deeply affected by an unfriendly legislation? I'm thinking for example of the Special Economic Zones Act (2005) or, for different reasons and cases of enforcement, of the various Armed Forces Special Powers Acts (1958, 1983, 1990).**

GND: It needs be understood that the basis of the 'Criminal Tribes Act(s)' was not moral. These Acts, beginning with the 1871 CTA, were not made in order to rescue humanity out of degradation. They were a cumulative result of various steps towards suppression of perceived/potential risks to the 'society' that had accepted the normative framework of the British Raj. Thus, the primary interest was to keep the social order safe, for the colonial rule was justified as a 'giver of law and order' to India. The Forest Act had to be brought in not because the Indian forests were dwindling. Had they really been facing the risk of depletion, sports like *shikar* and tiger-hunting would have found no support in the colonial notion of leisure. The primary aim was to bring under the government's command a valuable source for ship-building, timber. Hence, a special forest authority and code had to be created and the concept of forests as 'productive sites' had to be popularised. This was a big shift from the idea of forest as 'sacred zones'—under divine control rather than the regal order—that Indians had traditionally valued. Land, forest and the subject population—all of them—were for the colonial rulers a single spectrum of a larger economic activity which brought wealth to England. And the laws regulating Nature and Man were conceived to serve that single goal. The more recent special economic zone (SEZ) activity, and the 'simplification of law' to support that activity, are of a slightly different nature. In the previous lot of Acts, law was worked to consolidate the authority of the State. In the legal network supporting SEZs, the primary idea appears to be effecting a transition from the authority of the State to the authority of Capital (or call it the Corporate).

RC: In the recent past, activists and political parties have made multiple attempts to address the predicament of Adivasis through mass protests and political activism. In some cases this has also led to armed insurgency struggles. At a certain moment it seemed that a way out of injustice and a possibility of freedom from feudal bondage was to be found only in the Naxalite movement, or in other similar guerrilla factions; but in the end, do you agree that this produced only a long series of brutalities and in certain areas the creation of a sort of perennial 'state of exception'[3] with the systematic violation of human rights?

GND: Naxalism is the name given to a mood of 'disaffection towards the State', particularly the one that promotes violence as the means of communication. Since violence is involved in it, it is not surprising that it meets with counter-violence from the State. On both sides, this has unleashed a protracted process of brutalisation, dehumanisation and an absurd lack of any desire for dialogue. This gives rise to numerous cases of affective victimisation and violation of human rights. On the other hand, it also gives rise to a destructive tendency, hampering the development of tribal villages, and to an exploitative leadership that is incapable of working the existing democracy to the people's advantage. It is a sad situation, and I hope it comes to an end through consultation, dialogue and respect for Adivasi dignity as well as respect for human life and civilisation.

The Long Agenda of Social Issues

RC: **As you said, both before and after Independence, Adivasis have also been the object of a well-meant affirmative action through a set of legislative acts aimed at protecting their cultural heritage and at promoting their inclusion in the social body (via, for example, the policy of special reservations for the Scheduled Tribes in education and government jobs). At the same time the general sensation is that the post-Independence narration of universal citizenship finds in the condition of the Adivasis its most acute and sour disavowal. What's your opinion on the quota politics and its application?**

GND: Affirmative action is a good idea, but its address has remained somewhat vague. For example, successive governments have been trying to cut down positions (vacancies) in category III and category IV services. Thus, 8 per cent positions are reserved for Adivasis; but precisely those positions where they would typically join are curtailed. It is the same with the field of education.

In Gujarat, where I have spent time with Adivasis for the last 20 years, there are seven million of them. But, for these seven million, there is not a single dedicated university. There are very few pre-college high schools for science subjects. Obviously, Adivasis do not get into engineering or medical colleges (in larger cities). So, we have favourable laws for reservation of seats in education and employment. But, the provisions remain inadequately used (or are used by the creamiest layers). But this 'quota' tends to become a volatile and emotional issue. The poorer sections among those that do not have the benefit of quota have a legitimate grouse against the quota system. This gets translated into a blatant stereotyping of tribals and contempt towards them. It is the same with the Scheduled Castes.

RC: In *A Nomad Called Thief*[4], you state that the upward mobility registered in recent years in Hindu-caste society has left a vacuum at the very base of the social pyramid and that the tribals are pushed, willingly or unwillingly, to fill that gap. Do you confirm this is still going on? And what do you make of the increasing application of caste paradigms to the social fabric of tribal communities? On more than one occasion, like in [the riots] in Gujarat in 2002, Adivasi people were even involved in communal atrocities, fomented by caste or religious extremism, traditionally alien to tribal social culture. What do you make of these episodes? And, in relation to this, how do you consider the coming to power of the BJP? Has this effected a change of political climate towards the tribals?

GND: Sociologists use the term 'Sanskritisation' for a commonly shared social process of ascension to a higher economic status. Adivasi communities close to urban (or urbanised) centres of economic activities are now widely affected by the tendency to 'Sanskritise' themselves. In my initial years of work with Adivasis,

I used to get deeply disturbed whenever I heard from them any indication or statement of desire for a lifestyle that was at par with the 'modern, urban, middle-class' style of life. I was keen that they preserve their unique social structures, their famed innate sense of equality, etc. Slowly, I started seeing the element of unfairness to Adivasis in my own response. I have now come to accept that it is by no means wrong for Adivasis to expect to get benefits of modern medicine, education, well-protected habitat, drinking water and leisure. But, this is not to say that either the Adivasis become like the others or the others become like Adivasis—and that is the only solution for removing the inequalities. I now believe that 'essentially Adivasi' is more of a mental frame—a matter of values and beliefs—rather than an 'ethnic' identity. So, I imagine some of the non-Adivasis may like to move closer to nature as Adivasis in remote villages are, while some of them will move into urban middle class. There is no harm if the borders slacken.

The induction of Adivasis in the riots in Gujarat was a political advantage drawn upon the newly emergent desire to Sanskritise. But far more important is the fact that at the root of their unfortunate involvement in riots was their being lured by the moneylenders to whom they were indebted. Much of the 'involvement' was under coercion and not as a clear acceptance of the politics of hatred and violence. Soon after the riots, in the Assembly elections, the percentage of the Adivasi vote to the rightwing party was way below what it won in the urban centres.

RC: **And what about the very delicate religious question, both with regard to Hinduisation and Christianisation**

of Adivasis and their episodic involvement in religious fundamentalism?

GND: The worst loss for the Adivasis, due to the transition through which they are passing, is the erosion of their idea of the sacred. They have not known organised religion. They have not known patterns of worship with a godhead or where a god's representative is cased within a man-made building, a temple or a church. For them, being with nature in itself has been a form of worship. When they shift to faiths with a different idea of prayerfulness, the most inspiring notions of sanctity and divinity preserved in their practice, memory and word stand the risk of being wiped out. But as affiliation to various other religions in the country imply political affiliation too, by and large, the Adivasis who lose their own moorings tend to freewheel and gravitate close to those religious groups that have a political ascendancy. Alas!

RC: **Gender is another topic which seems relevant with regard to the social pressures which the Adivasis are experiencing nowadays. Is it true that the regime of relative freedom and social dignity that, at least in some groups, the Adivasi women were able to enjoy is increasingly threatened by new forms of gender discrimination deriving, at least in part, from caste politics and the fact that women are easily targeted by police repression or political organisations trying to make electoral inroads among the tribals by every possible means, intimidation and rape not excluded?**

GND: The most conspicuous is the fact that Adivasis whose land is reduced (every passing generation) due to indebtedness, unfair practices of external agents, multiplication of claims on land within the family, tends to treat the woman's body as a replacement of land. I have known hundreds of young Adivasi women who were asked to shift to nearby cities just a day after their weddings, and get working on construction sites. This is done, apparently, to recover the sum of dowry paid by the bridegroom to the girl's family. But, in effect, the girl becomes a construction labourer and has to work in harsh conditions till the sum is gained from her wages. The body has now replaced land as a means of production. This situation has come to a boiling point and may soon explode in the form of a movement for women's rights. I hope it does and changes the situation of the Adivasi women. I have spoken to a large number of Adivasi men to pay attention to this issue; but normally I have met with a cold reception from them, even those who I have known as friends and colleagues for two decades. Perhaps, an external feminist leadership is required.

Between Development and 'Slow Violence': Economic/Ecologic Issues

RC: **In post-liberalisation India, the traditional areas of tribal settlements have increasingly become key sites of economic development and infrastructural modernisation. To make way for industrial corridors, mega-dams, attractive installations or parks that essentially benefit transnational corporations and the metropolitan elites, tribal communities are continuously displaced and, without a serious relocation policy, very often left completely deprived of their livelihoods. Bonded labour, begging, pilfering, and prostitution are common ensuing phenomena. Besides, another effect of 'development' is the kind of delayed destruction which**

contaminates habitats and affects the very possibility of survival, defined by Nixon as 'slow violence'[5]: a violence that occurs gradually and usually out of sight because it is perpetrated in rural areas and without media coverage. In all this, do you think that the role of the forest tribes is only that of casualties, or do you believe that, defending themselves and their lands, they could possibly become active actors of a new conception of sustainable progress, respectful of environment but at the same time also of their economic needs? I mean, don't you think that to fight against the exploitation of natural resources without being able to provide new schemes of ecological development is too weak a position, liable to be easily defeated? Don't you think that in the future of Adivasis there should be a key role for technology? On the other hand, is it true that sometimes Adivasi people have found themselves in the position to compete with protected species and protected areas for their livelihood? What's your position in relation to this sort of apparent contradiction?

GND: I am acutely aware of how severely marginalised and cornered the Adivasis feel in the context of a market driven and globalised economy that has multiplied inequalities of all kinds. I have seen at close quarters the devastation caused by the sheer incompatibility between the tribal ethics and the modern economics. In the case of tribals (as in the case of Scheduled Castes and farmers), the intolerance is embedded in the economic outlook. But despite several thousand farmer suicides, the long-standing rural distress does not attract sufficient attention, and any movement of tribals is labeled 'anti-national' and at once caricatured as 'Naxalite' and dealt with brutally.

However, I do not think that violent opposition is the only means of opposition with the tribals. I firmly believe—and I have put this belief at the centre of all my work with the Adivasis—that violence can generate only a counter-violence and one that is far more destructive. On the other hand, aping 'caste India' can lead Adivasis to a complete destruction of their own culture(s). Therefore, it would be best to start (re-)building the Adivasi communities from within, to make them self-reliant, not dependent on government patronage or NGO alms. The ability of the Adivasis for deciding for themselves has to be enhanced. Let them decide what is good for them and what is not good. Then they will be able to cope *on their own terms* with the challenges and stress created by the market-led modernity. Sooner or later, this must happen. Sooner the better as they are rapidly running out of time.

Beyond Cultural Aphasia. Performing Indigeneity: Opportunities and Dangers

RC: **In the *People's Linguistic Survey of India,* the first comprehensive survey of Indian languages you supervised, you declared that, among other things, language is a marker of the welfare of a community. Bringing attention to Indian languages with small numbers of speakers, you said, is a way of bringing attention to the societies that speak them, along with the wellbeing of their people. With reference to the nomadic communities, what could you say in particular about the status of health of their languages and of their cultural identities?**

GND: The languages of the nomadic communities in India are among the most affected by the identity issues of these communities. Imagine any stigmatised community. The first thing that the community likes to do in order to secure its survival is to try and conceal its identity. Language is an identity marker for any community, but for nomadic communities it works as an identity marker far more pervasively. When these communities try to conceal their identity in order to escape the stigma attached them as 'criminal communities', one of the most obvious steps they take is to avoid using their language in the presence of an outsider. Thus they use a state language (other than their own) for all activities in which anyone from outside the community is involved, as in the market place, school, public places, etc., and they use their own language only among themselves, as a kind of a 'code language'. The natural consequence is that their own languages are getting skeletal by the day. In some languages of the nomads, the speakers no longer mention names of all seven days of the week or name more than two or three colour terms. Linguists will describe this condition of language as 'severe endangerment'. Recently, as I was preparing the People's Linguistic Survey in Maharashtra, I came across nearly a dozen DNTs (Denotified and Nomadic Tribes) that had great difficulty in recalling even a single song from their oral tradition. Maybe, about half a century ago, they had numerous songs and stories used on all occasions and social functions. This is so sad. This imposition of silence on those communities—forced because the stigma is not by their own choice—I call 'aphasia'.

Alas, so many languages are facing this threat. When the languages of communities are treated as a liability, the communities, too, tend to become economically further disempowered. One marginalisation adds upon another, cumulatively turning such people into 'the scum of the world' whose life is worse than that of beasts. This is a 'lived experience' of the communities and far more worrisome than a 'painful' theoretical position.

RC: **The predominance of orality in Adivasi culture and the lack of official institutions adopting tribal idioms for their activities seem to condemn the tribes to a condition of growing cultural aphasia. On the other hand, since Independence, tribal cultural heritage has repeatedly been paraded in State rituals such as the Republic Day celebrations or exhibited in State-sponsored institutions such as tribal arts museums or festivals. The existence of specific forms of knowledge and the relevance accorded to the arts are usually seen as the distinct mark of tribal contribution to the cultural mosaic of the nation. But, while for long Adivasi culture has been the passive object of ethno-anthropological inquest, more recently it has also become the privileged object of narration of artists who are also political activists, like Mahasweta Devi, Arundhati Roy, Laxman Gaikwad and many others, interested in defending the Adivasi way of life.**

What is more interesting is that nowadays it seems that many Adivasi artists are increasingly taking upon themselves the task of representing their worldview and asking, more than in the past, for a specific artistic recognition. I am referring to a whole range of experimentations with video-making and art cinema, or the output of a new literacy emerging from orality generated, for instance, after the textualisation of tribal societies in the wake of Christianity, like in the North

East.[6] But above all I am thinking of the performing and dramatic arts and the visual arts in which the tribals seem to find their favoured form of expression. See, for example, the great success of Warli art at a global level. Could you explain why? And tell us something about the role of the arts in your work with the Adivasis? And finally, what do you think about those who see in the national and sometimes international success of Adivasi artists, mostly painters, the danger of an evisceration of their cultural authenticity under the threat of commodification and desecration?[7]

GND: In 1998, I went to the Chhara ghetto (Chharas are a DNT community). Mahasweta Devi was with me. This locality is situated on the outskirts of Ahmedabad (not too far from the Sabarmati Ashram where Mahatma Gandhi lived from 1917 to 1930). No one from the city of Ahmedabad was willing to accompany me as the Chhara locality (Chharanagar) was seen as a den of crime. That was the stereotype. With great difficulty, we could enter the ghetto. On repeated visits, I could manage to make a few friends there. These were young men and women. When I asked them if they required anything as a gift from me, they responded asking for a library. We managed to create a small library in one of the houses there. At that time we were fighting for compensation for the widow of a tribal killed in police custody. The Chharas created a play (in the street theatre genre). It became a new sensation in the theatre world. As they performed again and again, the group of actors widened. The Budhan Theatre took birth.

Over the last 18 years, this theatre has performed regularly and a wide range of plays, including by the Italian Dario Fo and the French Jean Genet. Hundreds of small groups spread over many cities throughout India have gone to them to learn theatre from them. A few of their actors have graduated from the National School of Drama; some have gone to England to train (and returned to their own theatre); some have taken to film production. Dakxin Bajrange, the lead person of Budhan Theatre, won the National Human Rights Commission's National Award for his autobiographical book (*Budhan Bolta Hai*, 2010) last year. Today, the world looks at Chharas as artists and not as criminals. Several research dissertations and books and articles have been written on the Budhan Theatre. For me, to be the cause for creation of the Budhan Theatre has been a source of immense satisfaction and a continued inspiration.

So, indeed, theatre, performance, cinema—these are the means by which the expression of pain of the DNTs can be turned into a creative energy that can challenge and change the society (without taking recourse to the violent ways of the Naxalites).

RC: Could you tell us something about the 'Adivasi Academy' experience?

GND: Over the last two decades, the Adivasi Academy has carried out several experiments in the area of Adivasi development. It has initiated major policy debates in relation to the economic, social and cultural rights of the DNTs and Adivasis. However, the vision inscribed in these experiments has always been that of the communities themselves. The campaigns and the enterprises were more oriented towards generating the process of self-reliance rather than achieving quantitative success. There has been a conscious attempt at recovering the cultural memory of the nomadic and Adivasi communities, and investing it into economic and social dynamics in such a way that culture could be 'monetised'. These experiments have, from time to time, faced the orthodoxy of funding agencies in that the 'projects' that could not promise a direct economic output were rarely supported by them. This has, however, been seen by the Adivasi Academy as an opportunity to become self-reliant rather than as a stumbling block in 'development'. It is therefore that the Adivasi Academy has not stopped functioning even for a day despite long spells of having no external funding support. Irrespective of the nature of the interventions, each and every intervention has been fully owned by the Adivasi and the DNT community for which it was conceptualised. This is probably the most significant and 'valuable' feature of the Academy's experimentation. It can therefore be replicated in the context of any community in the world which faces lack of access and marginalisation. Similar experiments elsewhere, taken together with the learning at the Adivasi Academy, will help us in developing the precise method of working out the conversion between economic capital and social capital.

RC: In your letter to the Sahitya Akademi returning the 1993 Award given to your book, *After Amnesia*[8], you write '... I do this as an expression of my solidarity with several eminent writers who have recently returned their awards to highlight their concern and anxiety over the shrinking space for free expression and growing intolerance towards difference of opinion'. To what particular conditions of 'shrinking space for free expression' were you referring to?

GND: Writers like Perumal Murugan had to publicly declare that he would cease writing. Thinkers like Narendra

Dabholkar and M. M. Kalburgi were shot dead. Activist Govind Pansare was killed similarly. Those who protested were hackled or humiliated in a variety of ways. Any public statement in favour of tolerance and inclusiveness of diversity at once generates massive ridicule in social media, with trolls forcing many to withdraw from Facebook or Twitter, faces of speakers are blackened publicly to silence them and to terrify their audiences, artists are told to march off to another country if they even murmur a protest—all these together led me to say that free expression has become difficult, a dispassionate and rational view of events in the country is under attack and any dissenting view is an invitation to getting ridiculed.

Notes

[1] '"Akademi has not stood up for beleaguered writers": Poet Keki Daruwalla returns his award', *Scroll*, 14 October 2015.

[2] Ibid.

[3] Giorgio Agamben, *State of Exception*. Translated by Kevin Attell (University of Chicago Press, 2005).

[4] G. N. Devy, *A Nomad Called Thief: Reflections on Adivasi Silence* (New Delhi: Orient Longman, 2006).

[5] Rob Nixon, *Slow Violence and the Environmentalism of the Poor* (Cambridge: Harvard University Press, 2011).

[6] Margaret Ch. Zama, ed., *Emerging Literatures from Northeast India: The Dynamics of Culture, Society and Identity* (New Delhi: Sage, 2013).

[7] Rashmi Varma, 'Primitive Accumulation: The Political Economy of Indigenous Art in Postcolonial India', *Third Text* 27(6): 748–761, 2013.

[8] G. N. Devy, *After Amnesia: Tradition and Change in Indian Literary Criticism* (New Delhi: Orient Longman, 1992; third edition Orient BlackSwan, 2017).

REFLECTIONS

10 Bhor

The Ghosts of My Childhood

Who struck the first settlement here at Bhor or why is difficult to say. That must be several thousand years ago.

There is of course the river, and on the south-western bank, a gentle incline rising some three or four kilometres into a hillock. Neither the river nor the hillock can be called impressive. The river Nira allows buffaloes, children and itinerant sadhus to have a quiet dip without much of a ferocious drag. And the hillock, locally called the Shankar Hill, allows the cattle and the cattle boys to go up and down it without causing any difficulty. Beyond the other bank of the river, the land is very gently undulating, marked by not-so-majestic mango trees. The other bank and this one are connected by a narrow bridge.

As a school child, I could cross the entire span if I ran fast enough before the other children finished counting sixteen, seventeen, eighteen, but as a very young child I was a bit scared of running beyond the bridge. For there were two high schools a little beyond the bridge, and for me they were the dens of the grown-up boys. Both were on the left side of the road. One was called Yellow School, for that is what it was painted—a deep earthy yellow such as would make you feel a little colder. The other, just a stone's throw away, had its facade and the entire plinth done in light black rock, which made you feel even colder. Both buildings were matchstick box in shape, except that the stone-wall school had fencing in the front, with a tiny garden, and a small water fountain that never ever sprayed. All children rather used the entrance at the rear end of the building. The best part of the school campus—shared by both schools—was the playground. It had the gymnastic frames for pull-ups and push-ups, and not so fine a *mull-khamb*, a pole or pillar used by wrestlers for training. But the ground was large enough for the more prestigious games of cricket, with three proper stumps and a real leather ball.

The less prestigious cricket wars were played on Shankar Hill. These featured wooden bats stolen from the washing tools in houses and rarely any stumps. The balls could be rubber balls, but the most popular one was called '*butch*', a heavy but small lump of tire rubber.

The younger children, who did not have the courage to mix with high scholars, played with the boys who herded cattle on Shankar Hill on a little plateau that it had. This they did only in the afternoons, for the mornings were strictly for having a dip or a swim in the Nira. From 10 a.m. to 4 p.m., the hours were reserved for getting flogged by the school teachers. The municipal 'School Number 2' had seven classes and four teachers. Any three of them taught, and the fourth one ran the school office.

The boys' section had three rooms, two on the ground floor and the third on the first floor of one flank of the building. The two rooms on the ground floor were split-level. So any two classes could easily sit there. Ditto for the second room, but this one had additionally an exit down to the backyard, euphemistically called 'The Ground'. Along the ground was a small and slightly raised platform used for sermonising the children. The best of the sermons were given on 15th August and 26th January.

Initially it was only on 15th August. Later 26th January was added to the list of annual ceremony days as an afterthought by the school authorities.

Pedas wrapped in white butter paper were given to us on such days, one per child. The teachers kept all the remaining sweets for themselves; there was a toilet for severe emergencies at one end of the ground. There, in the compound wall of the school, was a gap left during construction through which one could easily step out and run to the river, a kilometre away, for a late swim.

We had a picnic every week. We were taken to Shankar Hill to collect cow-dung and bring it back to school to do a fresh layering of the classroom floors. We all sat on the floor. There were no benches. The school had no more than seven or eight chairs in all, three for the three classrooms, one for the headmaster, and the remaining without any specific purpose.

Cricket and swimming in the Nira were not the only games we played. Flying kites, *hu-tu-tu,* which also came to be known as *kabbadi,* and *vitti-dandu* were among the other popular games. Girls, if they had not attained puberty, played *kho-kho*. But the most favourite was the game of chasing each other and beating each other with thin twigs of creepers that were known among the children as '*fok*'. The game was known as *fokalne,* literally, beating. And the child who got beaten had to accept to be the 'wife' of the boy who managed to *fok,* for a while, until the 'wife boy' managed to gang up with another more gifted one and intimidated the 'husband'.

Since each of the boys was either wife or husband on any given day, one had to invent ways of escaping quickly, if need be, so that the husband could be hoodwinked. This gave each boy a chance to familiarise himself with every lane and bylane of the village and made him a potential explorer. If one's house had to be reached from any point in the village, there would be numerous paths entering a house and exiting from its backyard, jumping over fences, climbing over the roof of one house, moving to the next, getting down and so on. The combinations were endless. This also gave each child a good inside view of every household. Every child knew the precise items of furniture in every house in the village and had good opportunities of picking up the spiciest gossip about every family. Bhor had no secrets to keep. And it was never dull even for a day for there was always something sensational doing the rounds—about everybody. For instance, as a child of eight or nine I knew the exact rendezvous of every girl and boy six or seven years older to me.

Bhor in the fifties did not have too many streets. One moved from the bridge to the market street. On the left was the bus-station; to the right was the tent used in the evenings as a cinema theatre. There was a small *nallah* crossing this street. The market street itself was about 12 to 15 feet wide, not more. The market street led to the Municipal Council Office (MCO), and then split into two. The one on the left of the MCO ended up nowhere and joined the bus route from Mahad to Pune a kilometre further down. The one on the right met the same road, but crossed it and reached the foot of Shankar Hill.

Just before the market street opened, if you turned right, you would get on to a street taking you to the Bhoreshwar temple. But before you got there, you had to pass through an arch, known as the Kaman, and a little open square. To the left of the square was the Bhor Palace—not an impressive one—and to the right was a well-built river *ghat*.

At the back of Bhoreshwar was a narrow lane that went straight up to the Shankar Hill. One could walk all these streets on a morning between breakfast and lunch and get back to where one had begun well before the lunch hour. And that is how everyone knew everybody else: caste, problems, secrets, failures, debts, bank balance, everything. Bhor was one extended family where everybody was in many ways either a wife or a husband. It was not a place for widowers. There were a few in the village, but they cropped up in conversations as examples of how they had tortured their wives and how the wives looked at them with contempt as they died. There were a few widows, too. But Bhor was a little more dominant with them, and these widows were soon brought into social circulation as the men in the neighbourhood volunteered and vied with one another to assuage the emptiness in their lives.

My impression of Bhor is that there was no place for lust in the social life of the village. Sex was more a part of a ritual than any passion. One had to participate in it where and when it was necessary to participate. The village neither censured it not celebrated it. It just noted all liaisons without any shock, scruple or surprise. Just as lust was fully domesticated there, so was vice. All men spent their evenings playing cards and betting on them; but nobody in particular stood out as a great gambler. And if men liked to drink, locally brewed wine and *bhang*, no one showed the traits of being an alcoholic. For splashes, they travelled to Pune, 32 miles away, and then came back a few days later to resume normal life in the village. This was not a place for any big passion. Even when quarrels broke out, as they frequently did, the immediate mediation of neighbours quelled them in no time. For instance, when a wife was annoyed with her husband for not allowing her to make enough pickle in the summer, the entire lane would know of this in less than an hour and wives and husbands from every family would visit the distraught family by the evening suggesting a dozen ways of mending the harmony. Even the royal family got to know on a daily basis all such matters.

Close to the Municipality Office was a public library, the only one in Bhor. And there were no fees. One could go there and browse as well as borrow books. I liked to borrow one story book in particular, for I liked to read that story again and again. But when my elder sister noticed that I was borrowing the same book over and over again, she scolded me and forced me to borrow *Tarzan*. I just loved it. And the many others which followed, including a serialised *Odyssey* for children. In no time I became an avid reader of books in that library. This continued till I passed the final school examination and joined high school. The rules of the high school were different and I could not remain absent as attendance was marked every day. The library was in a different direction from the school. So my reading came to an abrupt halt. The last book I read was a short biography of Abraham Lincoln in Marathi. Of course, till this time that was the only language in which I could read and write. I could speak Gujarati, too, but no other language.

The paddy fields emitted a fragrance that cannot be described in words. It was a mix of the fragrance of dew infused with the joy of new birth for every grain as the blossoming saplings swayed in the gentle, gentle breeze.

I knew all the ghosts in Bhor. One had taken residence on the large tamarind tree in the Amrai lane. It was known for its ability to hang upside down from the tree and catch every person passing under merely by stretching its arms, which were known to stretch any which way and to any length. The second one was subterranean. It dwelt in the mysterious step-well, built at one time to provide drinking water to Bhor but which had fallen into oblivion since the new water tank was created by the side of Shankar Hill. This one was not seen, not spotted by anyone, but it could see everybody. And so it lived in rumours. The rumour was that it had come out of the unhappy daughters-in-law who had killed themselves by drowning. The third one was really ethereal. It came out only at the time that the day met the night and wafted out as a peculiar aroma, strong, overpowering and quite depressing. No, it was not the aroma of any sapling or herb. It was a ghost. It was so for all of us, and if we had to pass it by we had to keep chanting Rama, Rama 21 times until we were well past that peculiar, depressing aroma. But it was indeed lovely to have ghosts around, for they made our gossip full of adventures that were never going to be attempted.

Small talk and minding other people's business were the favourite habits of the people of Bhor. And these would not allow space for any high passions. Such high passion broke out only once. This had nothing to do with Bhor. It was all due to Gandhi. A Brahmin from Maharashtra had assassinated him. The news reached Pune through radio by 6.30 p.m. At that time there were no families in Bhor that owned a radio. Telephone was a far cry. People returning from Pune brought the news to Bhor by dinner time. An hour later, the families on the fringes, mostly those living closer to Shankar Hill, and away from the palace, got together. They talked animatedly. The night was spent sleeplessly. The morning saw very little movement in the streets. Children did not go to schools. Men did not play cards or go out to work. Women did not cook. In the afternoon, the families close to Shankar Hill formed a mob and started torching houses. There were no places to hide. Everybody knew where the Brahmins lived. Every Brahmin house went up in flames. There were no public buses for fleeing the place. Neighbours provided shelter to those whose houses were aflame. Children slept where they could. Men and women watched the fury without a murmur. The orgy continued for four or five days. And then Bhor returned to normal, except that an invisible line had been drawn between the houses close to the palace and the houses close to Shankar Hill, and the fields that lay beyond.

Bhor went back to normal. But, after the burning spree, children went to two schools, depending on whether they were closer to the palace or closer to Shankar Hill. My parents were neither here nor there. They often liked to be seen cooking and sharing food with the Brahmins. But the Brahmins thought of them as Gujaratis. And when they tried to be sympathetic to the Shankar Hill people, they were seen as people with money.

Ours was not the only Gujarati migrant family in Bhor. There were eight of those. The head of one was a lawyer, and close to the socialists among the Congress. Another was a moneylender who had taken upon himself the title of 'Nagar Sheth' because he had been lending and then appropriating land; he was both loved and hated widely. One family was very poor and the man heading it was always out of work and depended on help from cousins. The head of another family, basically a caterer from Saurashtra, had become a priest and built a temple on usurped land, for in Saurashtra the title 'Maharaj' is used for both cooks and priests. My father and his elder brother, my uncle, and a cousin of theirs, another uncle, too, had all set up grocery shops. All these families were simply called Gujaratis. And the Gujaratis remained unaffected by the invisible line in post-Independence Bhor; and as a child born soon after the assassination I had no difficulty in getting entry into all houses, Brahmins, tinkers, potters, Muslims, night-soil gatherers, carpenters, tailors, goldsmiths and landlords. But, despite my nimble running from hearth to hearth and getting affection from everyone, the invisible line kept growing thicker.

When I was seven or eight perhaps and not yet into high school, some of my Brahmin friends asked me to join them for a new form of entertainment that they had recently become addicted to. This was to assemble in an open ground, stand in orderly rows, put on black caps, salute a flag and sing a poem, which incidentally had a great serenity and which said, 'bow to the motherland'. After the prayer, we were asked to obey commands such as '*daksh*' (attention) and '*aaram*' (at ease) for a while. Then the young men who worked as instructors had to give demonstration on how to use *laathis* (batons) for self-protection. This involved a movement which enabled you to turn your face in all four directions and wave the baton in a manner as if you were going to hit someone's head with it. The movement was comical and we children all giggled a lot; but it was useful training as this was a sure way of saving yourself from being named a 'wife' to another boy in the school. A lot of my Muslim friends, too, were interested in joining the fun, but they were not allowed inside. So they used to wait outside for me to finish, go out and teach them the baton charge.

The fun was good, until Raksha Bandhan. On that day, and again very soon, on the Dussehra day, we had to spend several hours in a house listening to a *pracharak* from the Rashtriya Swayamsevak Sangh (RSS)—who was way above the *pramukh*—who came from Nashik or Nagpur and lectured to us on the values of commitment and strategy to keep our identity as Hindus unassailed. I found this a bit unbearable for I thought the pracharak was being treated with a disproportionate amount of respect by the pramukh. And I did not feel the same delight in receiving the insipid bowl of rice-based soup as I had felt in receiving the *peda*s at school on 15th August. And I was not very happy that my Muslim friends were not acceptable to the pracharak. I therefore decided to drop out—not because I knew what I was doing, but because at home a new entertainment had arrived. This was a Philips radio.

There were three radio sets in Bhor. One was Marconi, ours was Philips, and I do not know what make the third one was. The radio station had started a programme called the *Binaca Geetmala* which played every Wednesday. And by sundown, when I returned from Shankar Hill after the game of cricket and as the lamps came on in the streets, the radio played lovely melodies. I recall two in particular. One was from a film called *Jhanak Jhanak Payal Baje*, which ran '*Nain se nain nahi milao*'—I was simply transposed by the alliteration and the melody. The other was '*Jaye to jaye kahan*' again with its slight alliteration, but more because they were in a language I did not understand. Elders told me that it was called Hindi. Hindi cinema, too, hit Bhor about this time. *Tufan Aur Diya, Mother India* and several others based on sentimental stories started showing, one every week. A new sentimentality was on its way in. This showed particularly in the songs that were sung in the Ganesha festival cultural *melas* and talent shows.

When I was eight perhaps, apart from the appearance of the Sangh, one more important event took place. It was a procession organised to mourn the death of Babasaheb Ambedkar. This was brief, abrupt and did not have too many people in the procession. But the 30 or 40-odd people that participated did speak to the observers and tell them that a mighty champion of their cause had gone. The dividing lines were becoming more visible.

A year later, or perhaps a year earlier, the R. L. Mills set up near the Bhatgar Dam had acquired a new technology. The mills started turning out resin-based materials for tents, bags and covers—all painted in very bright, electric colours. In our village these colours, for which there were no accurate words in Marathi, were simply called 'English colours.' These English colours, and the factory that produced materials coated with them, instantly became Bhor's symbols for modernity. A few English terms started entering the general conversation. A couple of families that had spent a short time in South Africa, for reasons I will never know, moved to reside in Bhor. They, too, brought a few English words, which were soon put in circulation in the small talk of the village. One was a family called Joshi, and they made Sai Baba popular. Every Thursday evening they would hold a prayer meeting which was simply called 'prayer' in English. It was another thing that Sai Baba of Shirdi had nothing to do with the English tongue. It was at this time, too, that a new teacher joined one of the high schools. Older children told us that he was so brilliant that nothing he said was understood by anybody. He brought in a few words, of which 'mental', meaning insane, was one.

By this time Bhor had started losing its traditional rituals and folk artists. The dividing lines in the society had made drummers staying close to the Shankar Hill a little less popular. It was only during the winter nights that one would hear the sound of their drums in the distance. Previously, on winter mornings, the Bhutyas used to visit our houses. They sang in strange and haunting tunes a saga of Chilya Bal, a child who was brutally sacrificed a few centuries ago for his resistance to foreign domination. The Bhutyas also invoked goddess Vaghjai. The Vaghjai temple was located way beyond Shankar Hill. But now, after the radio and Sai Baba, the road to Vaghjai had become a little difficult to access. For one thing, a cubical water tank had been built right in the middle of this country path; and then people had moved from using traditional footwear to rubber slippers, which had suddenly flooded the market, and which were not steady or strong enough to support the long walk.

Those long walks used to be lonely. They took hours, and although we walked some distance, the elders often picked us up and carried us on their shoulders. We also used to walk up to the Bhatgar Dam, if the class teacher agreed to take us out on the yearly picnic.

But as the rubber slippers, Sai Baba and the invisible social lines came up, families started spending much longer indoors. Meals were finished earlier than before. Children returned home for supper rather than eating in other houses and sleeping there. The radio in Bhor was soon followed by an uncommon prevalence of mosquitoes. The government in fact set up a Malaria Prevention unit, whose small office was filled with large paper cans containing DDT. And to escape the mosquito menace, families took to sleeping on the roof tops. As a child

I loved the bed heated by the day's sun slowly cooling off in the breeze that would set in by night. Lying on that soft warm bed, one could see the sky all lit up by the bright stars. One was particularly keen to spot the Russian rocket going off the moon. A hundred times I saw a bright dot moving at great speed in the hazy sky. But mother told me that I was only imagining it. This made me sad and angry. And so when she told us one day that a huge flood had hit Pune, I said in revenge that it was her imagination. But it was not so.

Indeed, the Panshet dam had burst, drowning large parts of Pune, taking many lives and destroying thousands of houses. For once, since the years of Gandhi's assassination, Bhor united as one. Trucks moved through the lanes collecting blankets, clothes and food for the affected. People gave everything they could. The emotion was so strong that almost overnight Bhor became an emotional extension of Pune. A year later, my father went bankrupt and we left Bhor for good, never to return there.

Someone, I never could figure out who, used to make up little limericks. And then in a few days they used to get circulated. They were silly little things, but for the children they brought momentary fun. There was one in which Shivaji was made to attack the people who took to their heals in the name of Allah; there was another that brought the names of Hitler, Savarkar, Subhash and Gandhi to rhyme with the names of very incongruous objects in such a way that Gandhi looked like a veteran egg-eater and Savarkar 'braver' than Hitler. I knew none of these names, but the limericks gave me an idea of history that was close to ridicule.

Of history, I knew two heroic characters: one was Shivaji and the other was Krishna. Both, in my childlike vision of the past, were full of wisdom. For valour, I knew only one, a certain shepherd or peasant woman who climbed down the sheer walls of the fort, because it was past dusk and the gates of the fort had closed, and there was no other way she could leave the fort and reach her village far below. I found her fascinating for, in her desperation to get back home to her family, she had no fear of falling from the formidably high ramparts. The fear of heights and depths kept me away from such adventures. But I liked to imagine that my body had become light as a feather, and as I jumped I could stay midair longer than natural objects do.

Of heroes, I knew one. His name was Nehru. My admiration for this man was awakened by elders who had told me that Nehru's clothes were sent to Paris for laundry. This made me conclude that this man was different. Another thing about him was an elephant that he had gifted to children somewhere, perhaps Japan but I am not sure.

Once Nehru was to pass by Bhor—not quite—but his journey from Pune to somewhere in the south had a halt some 25 miles away from Bhor, at Shirval. Many children older to me went to see him, to shake hands with him and listen to him. When they returned to Bhor in the evening, each was trying to tell with pride how close they had got to Nehru—nobody called him Panditji—and how remarkably fair-skinned he was. Most of these children belonged to the Shankar Hill side of Bhor.

A lawyer had learnt how to cast a spell on snakes. Whenever a snake was spotted, people surrounded him. He would use a few grains of rice dipped in *kumkum* to caste his spell. There were plenty of these. We had cobras, the black ones, and *dhamans*, heavy snakes about six to eight feet long that moved rapidly and could climb walls. There were also plenty of rat snakes. A cobra had started visiting our house. It mostly came up to the water tank. And when someone spotted it, it crept away. Neighbours said that it was an ancestor guarding the treasure hidden in the vicinity. Some digging took place, but no treasure was found. Instead, three or four rat snakes crawled out and tried to attack the labourers ferociously. One had to be maimed flat. The cobra continued its visits after a while. So we summoned Mr. Shankar-rao Dev, for that was the lawyer's name. He arrived with a red cotton scarf and his rice grain charms. We all gathered around him to see how his magic worked. After he had muttered his mantra, he asked us to place the rice grains along the cobra's trail. We did this most dutifully. The next day the cobra was seen in the bathroom, having entered through the hole at the bottom of the wall made as an outlet for water. We called Shankar-rao again. And again he gave us the rice grains to spread along the open gutter. We did this. Probably, it was these frequent meetings that led to a kind of a friendship between the lawyer and my father. And so when my father's grocery shop started making heavy losses, and the debtors started knocking on the door far too frequently, he took Shankar-rao's advice and applied in the Magistrate's court for insolvency. That was granted on a Thursday in November 1961.

Three days before the judgment, father and mother spent hours debating where to shift the family. Despite angry protestations by mother, it was desired that the family be shifted temporarily to Sangli, where grandfather—my mother's father—had a house. On Tuesday we packed what we could, set off and landed in Sangli. Two days later, our house (with the cobra and the mango trees) was to be auctioned. Shankar-rao suggested that father show it was already sold. A distant relative in Pune agreed to purchase the house, backdated. The debtors got the court judgment, and on finding that father had no property in his name, cursed him. Father was left a broken man, bankrupt, not knowing what he would do with life. And we were in Sangli, not knowing how to look forward to another day.

11 Education

Learning to Read and Lie

It is now over six decades since I entered my first primary school. This was in a village so tiny that everybody in it knew everybody else. Probably no one in the village of Bhor had been to a college, and the parents of most of the children had not been to a high school. The general education horizon of my village did not rise above the seventh standard, known in those days as the 'vernacular final'. Yet, in my recollection, there was a great enthusiasm about the idea of education. This idea had some very physical manifestations. One was the cane that my class teacher carried with him. He believed in using it in order to improve the education of the village. The other was the puja on *Guru Purnima*. This was a full moon day when all of us carried to the school some coconuts, lumps of sugar and flowers plucked off the neighbours' shrubs for offering as precious gifts to the man who dominated the worst part of my childhood dreams. And he accepted all of it with a natural grace.

On Tuesdays, we were sent off to the nearby hill, about a couple of kilometres from the school, to collect dung and, having collected and carried it back in baskets to the school, to give a face-lift to the mud floors with it. For the rest of the week we used to dig holes in the floor, and of course conceal them under our slates and books so that we could play marbles during the recesses. Twice every year, we were told to clip our nails, do our buttons, press our clothes by keeping them under pillows the previous night and be generally nice. For, twice a year, the School Inspectors visited the school. Though there was a general excitement about these visits, on the days they took place, these mighty fellows spent most of their time in the headmaster's office, working on records; and towards the end of the day—generally the time we were getting ready to sort out the day's enmities and friendships through blows and vows—they stepped in. Never did they sit down. The inspectors stood and spoke. Therefore the teachers also stood and spoke. We sat on the dung-plastered mud floor. Naturally, they all looked taller than they were, like trees do in winter evenings. We were asked to recite poems, do quick sums and resolve huge grammatical problems like identifying a noun in a phrase. Every time, at the end of it, the Inspector asked us to study more. We went through the motions of nodding, with a hand ready on the marbles in the holes dug during the day.

Education for us was exploring the underground while pretending to look to greater heights. In the seven years of my wonderful schooling experience I learnt two things. One was to keep looking at the teacher no matter what was going on in my head—I do not think I was aware of my 'mind' till then, the head was everything—and two, if I was really interested in listening to what was being said, to shut my eyes while listening so that not the slightest of what was said escaped my grasp. When wandering singers stood at the door every morning, I listened to them with my eyes shut. Never have I forgotten the speed, the rhythm, the twists and turns of the voice they used for the lines they recited and the tunes they sang. As for the teachers, I remember them as a white cap or a striped pajama or a moustache, but no words, no tone, no smile.

By the time I left the school, I had a good collection of marbles, of friends who had betrayed me and joined my enemy gangs and enemies who had crossed over to this side of my fantasy battles. Yes, and I could swim, run, play cricket, climb trees, ride bicycles, read, count and recite some tables, switch on the radio and find the AIR station of my choice with a frequency so and so, crop pictures of cricketers from weeklies without cutting my thumb with a razor, blow crackers during Diwali, fly kites, whistle tunes, fold clothes and press them with metal tumblers filled with embers, identify the polar star in the sky, tickle unsuspecting uncles and aunts by putting pointed paper sticks into their ears, do a good dung-plastering for the house floors, wield a broom and clean a small patch of ground for a little game of *hu-tu-tu*. And most of all, I had learnt to guess with accuracy the rise or fall in temperature of the spiky verbal exchanges between my mother and my father.

I had also seen one death, of my grandmother. She was already quite blind and bent and forgotten and a butt of jokes and generally taken for granted by everybody around. None of my four cousin brothers were able to say exactly how old she was, though all of them knew she was old, full stop. They all called her 'Bai'. And being the youngest in the large number of cousins, brothers and sisters, I was not really noticed by her as she had lost her sight much before I opened my eyes in this world. Thus, when she was gone, for me it was only a shifting of a bed in the uncle's house where she kept lying for years before the formal end. But, I realised that a death in the family means shaving off your head, a general appearance of remorse in the family, previously unseen relatives pouring in for days, elders making this an excuse to avoid their work, some ritual meals, a priest hovering over the half-doused fire, a generally different event. I liked the experience. It was somewhat special, not the everyday kind. What I did not like though was the acrimony that soon developed between uncle and father over the distribution of the silver left behind by Bai.

Dividing the silver plates and chains and spoons and attar-sprayers was easy, but not so easy dividing the silver-studded saddle made by my grandfather for his favourite horse. I had never seen my grandfather, except in one already worn-out group photo. He was dead decades before I was born. I had only heard stories of how rich he was. Elders used to say that whatever my father spent was all inherited by him from grandfather. By the time Bai died, father had managed to blow up all of what he had inherited. Now came the rather funny looking half of the saddle, with no horse to fit it upon.

To my nine-year-old head, father did not quite strike me as a good-for-nothing man. He was good, extremely good in one thing that I admired. That was the skill to tell lies. He could invent a lie in a fraction of a second for dodging an angry debtor or covering up any of his silly mistakes. And not being smart about many things in the world, he made those mistakes all the time. For instance, he would go to the cloth-shop to buy saris for my mother, but return without buying any—a mistake. Then, when the scolding flowed his way, he would begin by saying how the shop had no stocks—but she had seen them a few days ago—how the shopkeeper had gone off on an errand—but he was spotted by the neighbours as very much being in the shop—how he had to suddenly rush to do some unfinished work—but which such work under the sun?—how he had a terrible chest pain on the way—but you look fine, and see how much you ate during dinner... and so on and so forth. 'Really, I've been such a dud, I should have known!', his voice would scale up. I learnt from him the beauty of lies, and the courage you need to defend a lie as if it is the last truth in god's world. I picked up the skill in no time, and loved myself for having done so.

I discovered that lies can increase the scope of beauty in life. And the more purposeless they were, the greater the colourfulness of the world. In my head, the sun stood for truth, and the moon for lies. This made me hum tunes of songs which had the moon in them. No matter in which language, Gujarati, Marathi or Hindi. I knew no English song. In fact I knew no English at all, not even the alphabet. For learning that, I had to go to the school beyond the river. And that was several years after grandmother had died and father had managed to blow up the silver in the half saddle, like he had done earlier with grandfather's farms and gold. So for me, English and father's complete bankruptcy entered my life at the same time. This was a little after the monsoon was over, and the hint of winter was in the air.

So I left, empty-handed, the childhood village of dung and lies, of songs and the moon, of death and silver, for a city that was beginning to hear English words like 'city-bus' and 'milk-booth'.

I remember that we went in a *tonga* from the railway station to the temporary asylum my parents had decided to make our home. Our few bags and bundles were loaded into the front of the carriage. Mother, two elder sisters and I sat in the rear, facing the gradually disappearing railway station. Father followed on foot. I spent ten years in this city. The two sisters were married off during those years. Father deserted us and went off to live in an ashram. By the time I finished college, it was only mother and I who were left. For a while, in-between, three children of the eldest sister joined us for a year and a half when the sister died in an unfortunate fire accident. At the end of those 10 years, I was 20, had travelled out of Maharashtra to distant places like Delhi, Meerut and Pathankot, learnt to clean, wash, work, earn occasional wages, had befriended hunger, read biographies, novels, plays and dreamy poems, even met some foreigners once or twice, knew by heart the history of Europe, the World Wars, had picked up books by Marx and, in short, done all that makes a young Indian loner learn to appear momentarily self-confident. And, yes, I had tried to remain athletic, had learnt to walk straight, look into people's eyes when speaking to strangers, wish elders and seniors in good English, wear a neck-tie, and be formal and polite in speech on occasions that called for such decorum.

And, also, I had learnt to read every day on subjects that interested me. Twenty years later, a slim book of a critical essay that I wrote received the Sahitya Akademi Award.

12 Lagori

Growing Up

I do not recall since when I started looking at my body as *my body*, not *me*. The memory of childhood is thick with the warmth and touch of many bodies in the large family that had several elders, girls, boys, workers, cows, visitors and close and distant relatives, neighbours and frequently visiting itinerant singers. To be alone all by oneself was not part of this kind of arrangement. And this was no arrangement either; all this just happened in the course of time, with nobody responsible for it. In that arrangement, bodies came in and they went away. The arrangement continued as before. As we children were playing *lagori* (a game with flat slabs of stone piled up, for knocking the pile down, almost like my family), some relatively younger elder came to inform us that grandmother—father's mother—had died. We rushed to the room where her body was kept, waiting to be cremated.

I recall that it was not sadness that filled my mind, rather it was surprise. A body that moved, spoke, saw and smelt until yesterday had suddenly become still, with only a slightly rueful smile left stuck to the edges of its lips. There was a string of rituals that followed over the next several days. Since at least some of my siblings were uninterested in the rituals, we continued to play lagori. However, I became more interested in the pile of slabs and watched it come up and go down, slab by slab, as if rock and body were made of the same unsteadiness.

The growing up of my body was uneventful. The only events associated were the deep wounds I received when I fell into ditches with sharp objects such as broken glass or nails as I ran around, playing and unmindful. Those wounds took time to heal and left deep marks for years on the knees, forehead and feet. They reminded one that the body was hurt. Except for these episodes of pain, the body made no other claim on me. It grew up almost as effortlessly as the leaves of night grow on the tree of Time. It is probably because of the ease of growing up that in my mind pain came to be associated with the life of my body, as its invited guest.

After my parents left their village and moved to Sangli, I became quite seriously ill. Since they did not have enough money to get me treated at any decent hospital, I was serviced at a charitable Ayurvedic clinic that provided free medicine. The treatment required my emptying out all traces of food inside me. I went through the treatment without really knowing either the cause or the consequence of someone else treating this body that had already started looking like someone else, not me. The body's suffering did not diminish due to the treatment. I said to myself: Here is a guest come for a long stay. Let me allow the body to accept the visitation.

During the second year of my college life, I developed the habit of getting up early in the morning and hitting the college playground for jogging and exercise. This I started doing on the advice from a retired Army Major who had accepted to train me for the Services Selection Board (SSB) examination. I did the physical part of the training with sincerity, but I did all of it with my mind as the driving force, as my need. The effect of this workout was good, and soon the way I walked, the way I stood, carried myself, all improved. I noticed that I was being noticed. The SSB was cleared once at Meerut—that is how the city was spelt in those days—and then again at Bangalore. But when the call letter came from the authorities asking me to join the Indian Military Academy at Dehradoon, I decided to stay back and work towards the Civil Services exam, and later turned to literary studies. In a few years, my affair with my body ended and it agreed to take a backseat in my scheme of things.

W. B. Yeats said, 'Too long a sacrifice can make a stone of the heart'.[1] Though I am not in entire agreement with him, I think he has a point.

Yoga and things like that were in the air throughout my years of youth. There were quite a number of fraudulent god-men and women around in all those places where I spent the first half of my life. There were also others quite remarkable by their saintliness. In the Marathi language, there was a large body of 'not-so-front-rank' literature about the world outside and above the human world. In those years, the term 'yoga' was not widely used. But the practice of it was widespread. Several of my classmates and college friends often spoke of how the body can be transformed through *sadhana*. I knew their interests well enough. However, I always thought that the mind is closer to permanence than the body, and if one has to do any sadhana, it had to be more for the mind than for the body. My doctoral research was about a poet who had chosen to be a dedicated yogi, and his work convinced me that the life of the mind is much superior to the life called body.

However, the dichotomy remained subdued in my thoughts and did not trouble me in any degree comparable to what James Joyce's protagonist in *The Portrait of an Artist as a Young Man* had to suffer. It was when I was forty that entirely unknown to myself I started developing an as yet not experienced sense of freedom. In those years, I had acquired the habit of going for long walks. These were not walks in any health resort, walk-tracks, playgrounds or woods. I used to walk through the streets of Baroda, filled with crowds, shops, schools, temples, bazaars and stray cows. In the beginning I did not know why I felt so elated and so free as never before. But gradually, my thoughts started getting affected by this new awakening. I then realised that I was fast losing the fear of death. Together with it, I had also started losing interest in any kind of accumulation of wealth. I felt life would be just as meaningful were I to wander in the streets of India as a fakir, as, if I were to continue with my university professorship. When these thoughts multiplied in frequency and became very intense, I spoke to Surekha and shared what was in my heart and soul. I said, 'The time to quit has come'. She understood what I was trying to say. Since then, I have developed the habit of looking at pain and pleasure as expressions of the one and the same substance, and the body as the host for joy and suffering, an inviting host, never grumbling about the visitors.

After the age of forty, all my writings on literary aesthetics have been deeply impacted by this understanding of continuity. I know that when one slab of stone is knocked off the pile, another one rises to replace it. The 'lagori' continues even if a grandmother goes off. So it will be with me.

Notes

[1] W. B. Yeats, 'Easter, 1916'.

13 My 'Brahmin' Self

I started reading the poems of A. K. Ramanujan during the early 1970s, and was at once charmed by his description of his Brahmin self. In poem after poem, the irony of Ramanujan's wanting to belong, and not being able to belong, to his Hindu past led me to internalise some of my own predicaments in terms that were both modernistic as well as rooted in India's learning traditions. This was also the time when I had already read U. R. Ananthamurthy's *Samskara* and Raja Rao's *Comrade Kirilov*. Earlier, I had met Ananthamurthy and, on listening to him, had felt impressed by his admiration for some young Dalit writers. These three writers helped me in looking at my own cultural antecedents with all their complexities.

I grew up reading Marathi literature. Marathi was the language of my upbringing. The books I had read in Marathi were mostly written by Brahmin writers. Though, as a school-going reader I was not able to identify or name it, what left me cold about most of them was the unmistakable ethos of a 'Brahminical' sentiment. They had too many words and too little to say. The social sympathy about the poor, and whatever idealism that one came across in them, were somewhat distanced from the subjects depicted and had a certain superficiality. When I was fifteen, I came across Vyankatesh Madgulkar's

Banagarwadi. It hypnotised me with its simplicity of words and depth of sentiment. This book was about a village teacher who experiences the village by transcending all caste boundaries and learns to value human beings for what they are.

I was born in a village myself. This village had a certain predominance of Brahminical culture as it was ruled, till Independence, by a Brahmin ruler. Most of the educated persons—there were only two or three with a university degree—and even those who had been school dropouts spoke the Marathi language with a thick layering of Brahminical idiom. Their sentences were full of proverbs that reflected a deep inwardness to myths approved by Brahmins. Most of the school teachers, too, were Brahmins; and as such, most of the 'good' students picked up 'good' writing skills fairly fast.

Of course, there were persons from other communities as well who belonged to that village. My parents, who were not Brahmins though they liked to describe themselves as ones, tried to keep their children away from the gaze of these others. I saw them in the weekly bazaar. It took me no time to recognise that they spoke a Marathi that was remarkably different. Their language to me sounded closer to the smell of the chillies and onions that they brought to the bazaar for selling. The Brahmins in the village specialised in eating food that was relatively insipid and used garlic and onion in moderate doses. During the four months of monsoon they just desisted from using garlic and onion altogether. For a long time, I thought of the 'other' communities as the communities which smelt of garlic.

I had friends in school who belonged to the Maratha community. In my memory of the touch of their bodies, I associate them with painless bones. Their frames were bonny and their biceps were full. The Brahmins surrounding us had biceps that looked like a pencil, all smooth and evenly cylindrical. Besides, the Maratha boys did not speak like their sisters. They spoke like themselves, or at least like their fathers. My childhood quota of four-lettered words came in abundance from these Maratha boys. I had a Muslim friend whose name I remember as Roshan Sheikh. He was fair-skinned, somewhat fat and extremely affectionate. The most favourite pastime of the Maratha and the Muslim boys in the village was to articulate in every possible public place how they would like to sodomise the Brahmin boys. For quite a while I did not understand that this was a metaphor, a manner of speech rather than a statement of any real sexual desire. In any case, none of them was capable of sexual performance since most of us were yet under ten. However, when I was ten, I happened to overhear a conversation between a Maratha boy called Kisnya and another boy, whose name I do not remember, about Kisnya's sleeping with a rather robust girl called Kamli. His description was graphic. The other boy named another girl and asked Kisnya if he would not do 'it' to her as well. Kisnya said that he did not consider Brahmin girls worth his labour. This chance comment remained in my memory for a long time.

The games that the Brahmin boys played and the games that the others played differed, too. The others were interested in *kusti*, wrestling. The Brahmin boys mostly ended up joining the RSS *shakha*. I was taken there by one of my seniors. Initially, I found the idea of staying out of the house till well past evening very attractive. Also, I liked the tune of the prayer quite a lot as it reverberated through the quiet evening hour. But soon the teacher—whom we called Guruji—started telling us how the 'circumcised ones' had been a bane to India. At that time I was not interested in thinking about India. Besides, I was interested in my arguments and subsequent compromises with Roshan Sheikh. So, I dropped out of the shakha.

Myths, festivals, gods, clothing, speech, food, occupations—all of these marked the Brahmins of that village as different from the Marathas and the Muslims. There was yet another community called Bhoi, which remained on the last social periphery of the village. For the first ten years of my life, my parents brought me up under the illusion of being a Brahmin, or at least close enough to being one. But something happened in my family and my parents had to leave the village. The happenings were so drastic that even to mention the village in our conversation became painful to all of us and, as a family, we started trying to root out of our beings traces of the past. My parents had great difficulty in managing to do this. But as I was only ten at that time, this was easier for me to do.

The first thing that happened to me after we left the Brahminical village was that I was allowed to see a movie all by myself. The first such movie I saw was *Junglee*. The lead actor in it was Shammi Kapoor. His entire body language was unlike that of any of the Brahmins I had seen in the village. I found the songs in the movie as well as the body language of this man with a rather unusually large face extremely unlikable. In comparison, I liked Saira Bano who had paired with Shammi in it. Soon after, I joined a school that was established for educating children of the Wodder community. These were a community of stone-crushers whose men were dark as night and whose women did not wear blouses. Their language—a strange mix of Kannada and Telugu—was stunningly vibrant. I immediately fell in love with their ways. I did not know at that time that the term 'culture' could be applied to describe their ways of eating, quarrelling, abusing, beating, shouting, crying and running after a person in a wild chase.

The teachers in the school, even this school, were all Brahmin, except one who had recently deserted the army and had taken up teaching as a profession. He tried to look like Shammi Kapoor and between teaching us geography and physical training, chased a lady teacher. It was here that I started reading books, obviously books in Marathi as that was the only language I could read or speak. Most of them had a terribly suffocating Brahmin ethos as the backdrop. Therefore, I turned to Marathi translations of European and English classics, biographies of great characters in history, and *Tarzan* comics. I enjoyed all these immensely. But, in school a Brahmin teacher decided, for reasons I have still not understood, to teach us the *Gita*. We were made to memorise the fifteenth chapter of the poem. I managed to memorise it not too well, but a shade better than what the Wodder students could do. Forty-five years later, I can still recite the verses, though I have never experienced the desire to understand the meaning of the fifteenth chapter even when I started looking at the *Gita* in a serious way some 15 years ago.

The college I joined after my matriculation was in Pune. Here, too, I found that most of the teachers were Brahmins. As a result, though I had been quite a good student during my school years, I now felt that I should rebel against the authority of the teachers. I did so, and suffered badly in the examination at the end of the first year. This led to my leaving that college and joining another college in Pune which was dominated by a heady mix of Christians, Parsis and Iranian students. By now I had started making attempts at reading books in English. But my English was so inadequate that I started feeling a sense of inferiority in this new college, and I left studies altogether.

My elder brother brought me back to studies, this time to the study of English literature. Here, too, the teachers were again all Brahmin, but the principal of the college was a non-Brahmin. I had heard that he drank regularly and even visited inexpensive sex workers. At this stage, I got interested in Hindi cinema music and started singing for myself all those songs. The reading of English books, singing of Hindi songs and my short-lived interest in an armed forces career helped me quite a lot, for the first time in life, to be myself. By the time I graduated from

Willingdon College, Sangli, with a B.A. in English, I thought I had managed to get rid of the Brahmin coating given to my person by my early childhood days in the village I have earlier described.

At the university, I came in contact with a Jain professor who was also a modernist fiction writer. He wrote in Kannada. The university where I studied was located in a predominantly Maratha cultural milieu. It provided a wide berth to all other backward communities, too. Here I met a very beautiful girl, who agreed to marry me. She came from the Lingayata community. By now I had acquired friends who were attracted by the ideas of Karl Marx. And the People's Publishing House outlet in that town brought to me low-priced editions of revolutionary literature. All these factors gave me a great sense of relief. I felt I had finally found myself.

It was at this stage that I came across the works of Ananthamurthy, Ramanujan and Raja Rao. It was also at this stage that I started reading Sri Aurobindo, placed side by side on my book shelf with works of Marx and Freud. I then knew that the Brahmin in the Indian consciousness is like some permanent colour-fast substance. At this stage, I was getting interested in understanding the political dynamics between the Marathas and the Brahmins, and I realised that I could not fully sympathise with either of the two sides. I felt I was an alien in this city; the political debates and tensions there felt very unreal and remote to me. Though this was the place that gave me my first taste of rich non-vegetarian cooking, I did enjoy a sense of superiority that my Marathi speech gave me over the others. And, even if everybody there mistook me for being a Brahmin, I had already acquired several marshal qualities due to my brush with the army to not allow myself to feel like a Brahmin. I knew that the Brahmin has been an uneasy presence throughout the history of this country.

14 Seeing

Through the Eye of the Peacock Feather, and Charlie Chaplin

My life has been lived through my eyes, not so much through the ears, touch and taste. So very often even before the person in front of me has started the conversation, said what is to be said, concealed what is to be concealed, tried the artful deceit or effusively claimed a non-existent momentary kinship, or just plainly placed facts, enquiries and questions before me, my eyes seem to grasp it all, or almost all, before words frame those thoughts and convey them to me. So very often my colleagues and friends tell me how greatly intuitive I am, which I am not. It is just that my eyes work a wee bit faster than the rest of my cognition. They grasp things faster than my mind does.

When I was younger, I would occasionally look at my eyes in mirrors and try to see what colour they were. It was not easy for me to decide if they were dark, light or some shade in-between. I recall that such moments of looking at my eyes made me for those moments quite empty. My mind would cease to register anything at all, including the act of my looking. I no longer have a clear memory of the experience, for I am now at an age when I can hardly see my eyes, or myself, in mirror images with any clarity; except occasionally in the concave mirrors of hotel bathrooms and in the side-view mirror of my car when I drive. I no longer have much idea of what colour they are. I do not really know what they are like. I have known the world through a part of me that I used to know uncertainly, and no longer know except in rare moments of narcissistic self-examination.

I have with me quite a collection of spectacles that I have used over the past 20 years. Rarely have I discarded the old pairs. All of them sit on my study table and I try them out even if my sight has dipped a little and acquired a higher number. All these spectacles have been, at different times, intimate parts of my knowing and the material extensions of my seeing. These, too, I have not observed with any great care.

Homer, Surdas and Milton, the greatest among the poets, fascinate me for their blindness. Sanjaya of the *Mahabharata* and Cassandra of Troy fascinate me for their ability to see more than their sights would allow them to. I think the world can be seen only by those who cannot see at all or by those who can see even when they are not seen to be seeing. My experience of life has been through such seeing. Therefore, where there is time, I see space, where there is motion, I see stillness, and where there is silence, I see voice. It is in my seeing that my mind has felt spurred or stalled, driven or drawn, illumined or blocked. It is as if I have been a brainless being, but like a hundred-eyed hydra, my mind has been all eyes. Knowing for me has been seeing, though my seeing has remained largely unknown to me.

My earliest memory of my eyes is related to train journeys. In those days, soon after Independence, the tracks were in most cases narrow-gauge and the engines were fuelled by coal. The window shutters were normally left open and children put their heads out of the windows to admire the landscape or, if the windows had any grills, kept their faces pressed against the iron bars. The speed of the train made the coal dust fly backward and the particles entered one's eyes. No matter what you did, washing the eyes with water, rubbing them or blowing moist air against them, nothing helped and the pain and discomfort continued till you ended the journey. This is exactly how I have passed through life, seeing and feeling hurt.

During my school days, peacock feathers had a special value. One often presented a feather to one's dearest friend, and if the friendship floundered after a few weeks, one would promptly ask for the gift to be returned. Such feathers were kept in our favourite books with as much care as, I imagine, emperors kept their precious treasures. The peacock feathers so acquired—kept and brushed a thousand times against one's cheeks, felt and smoothened with one's palms—were believed to have eyes. I was more than convinced that a feather hidden in the pages of the book would read the page and the entire book and store all the lines in its head—I imagined that the eye of the peacock feather had a head of its own. From these feathers, I learnt the art of reading books with a rapidity that was uncommon for someone like me with not such a brilliant performance in school examinations.

I had seen elders and my teachers holding the pages of a book they read tightly between their thumbs and the other fingers. I figured out fairly early in school that it is possible to scan a page with the rapidity of a peacock feather's eye. This soon became a habit for me. There was a small public library in my village created towards the end of the nineteenth century in memory of a lady from the royal family that held the village as its estate. The library was not too far from home. I was introduced to it by one of my elder sisters. I would pick a book from the library, hold it before my eyes and walk home reading it. By the time I reached home, I would have completed reading it, and would walk back to the library to return it. Having invented this method of reading, it became easy for me to remember what was in the books I read, and generally by the page numbers as well. And once read, a book would sit in my head—the head of my eye—for years and decades.

I was not aware that there is such a thing called reading speed till I heard for the first time from someone that there is a skill called typing which is measured in terms of the words typed per minute. This was when I was studying in high school. I had not then actually seen what a typewriter looks like. I had to take an eight- or nine-minute bus ride to reach the school, two stops away from home. I remember going over 80 pages of a Marathi book—the only language I had learnt till then—during a single journey. This did not require any effort from my side, nor did such an experience leave me fatigued.

When I entered college, my ability to write, speak or understand the English language was comparable to that of a new literate person. The inability to write effectively in English was one of the reasons—among others—for my decision to drop out of college and start looking for a job. Obviously, there were no jobs suitable for a 16-year old not knowing a language beyond Marathi.

During this phase, I had taken residence in a village in Goa, and there existed a very small public library with Re 1 as the monthly fees. There I chanced upon a copy of *The Good Earth* by Pearl S. Buck, an American novelist quite popular in those times. I had to struggle with it, using an English–Marathi dictionary. But a couple of weeks later, I picked up another book, *The Guide* by R. K. Narayan. Having earlier seen a Hindi movie based on the novel, I could make good progress through its pages. It was then that I decided that I could actually read and understand English fiction. This led to my joining college studies again—this time to study English literature.

As was the practice in those years, a fairly large dose of nineteenth-century writers, from Thomas Carlyle to Thomas

Hardy, had to be studied. I do not quite clearly recall when, but probably a year later, I concluded that I could pour over about three hundred printed pages of English on a good day, and decided that I would make this my normal practice. With rare exceptions, I followed this practice till, at forty-three, my first book in English was given the Sahitya Academy Award in the category of books in English. By forty-five, I decided that I would give up reading books. This decision was triggered by my resolve to move out of the university and go to Tejgad, a tribal village. It is not that since then I have not read any books. That I have done once in a while. Besides, I have been reading newspapers fairly regularly and have read essays, book chapters, reports and things like that. But I have not kept up my reading habit of earlier years when I would consume a book or two or even several of them every single day. All of those books I read with my 'peacock feather eye', scanning the pages and avidly stocking everything in the mind of that feather, available to my recall whenever I required anything from it, but without ever bringing to *my* mind the awareness that I was well-read.

After completing my doctoral work at Kolhapur and before taking up a teaching job in Gujarat, I spent a year at a British university studying poetry. Given how little is taught there and how few lectures one is required to attend, a lot of my time was spent in the large library available there. Generally, I would go to the library as its first visitor and stay in for as long as I could. In between, if I went out for a cup of tea, I visited a student cafeteria. In this cafeteria there was a remarkable range of paintings done by a former student or a local artist. The paintings, all of them, depicted scenes from various films of Charlie Chaplin. What struck me most about those paintings were Chaplin's eyes. The deep dark collyrium-lined eyes of this wonderful artiste were used in those images as his way of looking at the world. Here, for the first time, I started thinking of activism. My early childhood train journeys with coal-hurt eyes and Chaplin's eloquent, heavily-kohled eyes stood in sharp contrast for me. I understood that social problems and rights issues cannot be seen merely as the bothersome unwanteds of history. They need to be looked at critically, with defiance and even contempt, but not without compassion for the victims as well as the perpetrators. Sitting there in that cafeteria, I decided to borrow the Chaplin eye. Subsequently, my chase for Gandhi's idea of the world made the meaning of Chaplin's defiance clearer to me.

When I decided to stop reading books, and as the peacock feather stuck to my eyes from my school days dropped off, I noticed that the Chaplin eye was waiting inside to take position. The activist work that I undertook at this stage was carried through entirely on the clarity of the vision illumined as well as occluded by the Chaplin eye that I had made mine during my days in Britain. Many of my friends have asked me how I have been able to conduct myself as an activist without getting visibly angry. It is not that I have managed to free myself from anger. In fact, in my personal life I have had to regret violent bouts of anger on numerous occasions. But the eyes through which I approached the tribal communities, there was no space for any flashes of anger in them.

Ananda K. Coomaraswamy's *The Dance of Shiva* has been one of the most fascinating books on literary and cultural theory. Coomaraswamy was an outstanding commentator on ancient Indian iconography. His description of the dancing Shiva makes a compelling read. Yet, despite my admiration for the depth of his understanding, I have always felt—and this is in an entirely irrational way—a bit distant from Coomaraswamy. I have always wished that he had picked up a different focal symbol and a different title for his book and not that of Shiva in a nihilistic mood. Shiva with his third eye awakened may be a great symbol. My normal intellect and normal mind accepts and understands that symbolism. But I wish we had a Shiva with his eyes closed—as they normally are through the aeons—who intuits the end of the world rather than effecting it though an 'eyeful dance'. This, I am aware, is only a fantasy related to our mythology.

My acquaintance with the Sanskrit language has been scant and discontinuous. The first time I was made to utter words and sentences in Sanskrit was when I was in middle school. A teacher decided to get us to recite the *Bhagwad Gita*. He chose the fifteenth chapter and asked us to cram the first ten verses. All of us did this as told, more out of the fear of punishment rather than any great love for the language. The motion of reciting was purely mechanical, and we hardly understood any lines or words. Yet, the last line of the tenth couplet startled me. It reads: '*Vimudha nanu-pashyanti, pashyanti gnancakshu-shah*' (He who knows not does not see, but the one who sees with the 'eye of knowledge' knows). The idea of an 'eye of knowledge' caught my imagination and I made what was an easy conclusion for me at that age: know with your eye so that you are less foolish.

Often in my career as a literary scholar, friends and admirers have paid compliments on some of my work. It is a normal practice among the community of scholars to flatter others in a face-to-face conversation. 'Insightful', they have said. I know that such praise is to be responded through complete silence, in humility. But every time I have heard the epithet, my mind has recoiled. I clearly know in my heart that I never had any insights, nor will I have any. 'Sightful' would have been a more realistic description of whatever I have done. For, all my life I have done nothing at all, except allow my eyes to be the superior of my mind and head.

Once, a Maharashtrian lady decided to write my biography. A friend said to me, 'Won't it be much better if you write your own story, an autobiography?' I know that I shall never write my autobiography. I just cannot. For I know with utmost clarity that I shall never be able to tell myself what enabled me to see what I saw and the way I saw. Even if I try again and again at different times, I end up seeing the same space. It is the same space in different times, the same thought in different minds, the same continuity in different ruptures. Almost entirely, the ideas that I can call mine, the flashes of realisation that fell into my lap, the strangeness of things that appear in my writings, the actions I planned and executed in my work related to Adivasi communities, and the manner in which I have conducted myself and understood myself—all of these have been a result of my seeing, without seeing how I see.

The unblinking gaze stares at life as a perennial witness of the million shifts, transformations and changes without allowing the mind to know that it knows. I seem to have lived my life through my eyes, and therefore, neither knowledge nor action has ever been a burden to my mind.

15 Of Heroes Fabled and Ordinary

Shivaji Maharaj was my undisputed hero from the time I joined the primary school till I entered the university in Kolhapur named after this epoch-making persona from the seventeenth-century history of western India. During Diwali, we used to build tiny mud-castles outside our houses and adorn them with terracotta figurines of Shivaji's soldiers.

I heard of Dr. Babasaheb Ambedkar for the first time when he died. At that time I was not old enough to know much about him, but I gathered through the talks of the elders that he was a follower of the Buddha and had written the Indian Constitution. I felt this was a different kind of a hero. Both Gautam Buddha and Babasaheb occupied a large space in my imagination.

In the last year of high school, I read about the Italian legend Joseph Mazzini (not so much about Garibaldi). He and Subash Chandra Bose fascinated me. So did Abraham Lincoln. I had read in Marathi translations biographies of some of the great men and women of history. The valour of the Rani of Jhansi and the tragic death of Lincoln overwhelmed me.

When I was sixteen, a second-year college student, I chanced upon a book by a Japanese war veteran. This man, his name was Saburo Sakai, wrote about his days as a fighter pilot in World War II and of his values as a samurai. For a while, he became my hero. Twenty years later, I visited Japan for the first time. I asked several of my friends there if they knew anything about Saburo Sakai. They all looked at me with blank faces. I surmise that it was probably an American pulp fiction book that I had credulously taken for a life-story.

During my first year in college, I came across the Marathi translation of Arthur Koestler's collection of essays, *The Yogi and the Commissar*. I had read a lot many books in Marathi by then, but had not read anything in that genre. It mesmerised me so much that I read and re-read the book literally every day till I remembered every sentence in it. This experience brought me to the realisation that heroism is as much and even more a quality of the mind. I should add that when I tried to read this work 20 years later, I could not stay with it beyond a few minutes.

At this stage I was reading Thomas Carlyle's *On Heroes, Hero-Worship, and the Heroic in History*. I recall that I was not able to share his passionate admiration for the heroes he had chosen, but I did find some elements of his style admirable. The hyperbole at its best was a new rhetorical possibility for my adolescent mind. I also found Oscar Wilde's epigrammatic prose alluring. The range of my heroes was expanding.

The Marathi idealist writer Sane Guruji—he ended his life out of despair—was a great attraction for me. Though the regional novels and the historical fiction left me cold, I absolutely liked the rural realism of Vyankatesh Madgulkar. For reasons rather strange, I turned to the German and French philosophers towards the last year of my college. The reason was my inability to admire historical characters such as Napolean and Frederick the Great. Nietzsche and Spinoza were more assuring. So were their ancients, the Greeks Plato and Socrates.

Shakespeare was charming, quite contemporary, and Ibsen, at least for a while, was attractive. The range kept widening, bringing in more German writers—Herman Hess and Thomas Mann, Kafka—more French writers—Camus, Jean Genet and their seniors Flaubert and Andre Malraux—American writers—Hemingway, Malamud, Arthur Miller—and, of all, the great Russians Gorky, Tolstoy and Dostoevsky, so also the unparalleled Irish geniuses Joyce and Yeats.

In those years, my mind also provided a hospitable abode to many of the ancient and medieval Indian story tellers and poets: Vyasa, Kalidasa, Bhavabhuti, Mira, Tukaram, Kabir and, of course, our own Tagore and Premchand, to name only a few. Literature available in English translations from other Indian languages was steadily increasing in range. I could also read in the original Hindi the remarkable works of Phanishwarnath Renu, Srilal Shukla and Nirmal Verma. Perhaps, between the ages of 15 and 30, my ideas of heroism had changed so radically that if I had to think of my thinking, I preferred to fall back on the thinkers, dreamers, poets, dramatists and visionaries rather than on kings and warriors.

As the years passed, I started looking at film-makers, painters, architects and musicians as well for constructing my self-image. Their colours, tones and shapes, too, provided easy tropes for identifying my own mind-scape. It was as if one could access a vast collection, an eclectic one surely, of minds—from Freud to Ritwik Ghatak, from Antonin Gaudi to Shivram Karanth, from Strindberg to Solzhenitsyn—for describing 'my' mind.

About the time I was thirty, a huge wave of sleekly produced books in a newly developing area called 'theory' started pouring into the academic book market in the United States and the United Kingdom. A decade later, they had found their way to the Indian book market as well. These had titles in English translation by Levi-Strauss, Derrida, Foucault, Lyotard and many others. As I used to visit the Western universities quite frequently during the 1980s, I quickly made a good collection of such titles and poured over them. Their brilliance and intellectual range were always amazingly impressive. However, as I was myself actively developing my own ideas, I do not remember having been particularly influenced by any of them. At best they could be my friends, but neither my lights nor my mirrors.

It was when I was in my mid-thirties that I gradually realised that there were yet more difficulties in describing myself. These were not difficulties arising due to any shortage of tropes. It was rather out of a moral inadequacy. This new hindrance was caused by an old man called Mohandas Karamchand, known to the world as Mahatma Gandhi. Somewhat uninvited, he started appearing in my thoughts, and with every appearance he made, made me feel somewhat incomplete, and shorter than I had so far imagined myself to be. Exorcising this ghost was a tough job. It took me nearly 20 years of work with the poorest of the poor to get back on my own feet. It also meant cleansing myself of all traces of literary learning. That is, of course, another story.

My difficulty with Gandhi was that all along I had prided in my independence. Despite my close study of Sri Aurobindo I had managed to retain that independence. Neither Marx nor many of his variants in modern Indian history had succeeded in enslaving my thinking. But Gandhi was really enigmatic. Because his thought was neither rooted in logic nor in ideology, it was difficult to quarrel with him using arguments or by taking reasoned positions. He was neither brilliant nor overwhelming as a hero. At best, like the portraits in Bhupen Khakhar's paintings, here was an unattractive person who could raise X-ray sharp questions.

During my work with the nomadic communities and Adivasis, Gandhi remained with me like an inseparable umbrella. However, slowly, very slowly, I started realising that just as he was in the habit of getting into your mind, he also allowed you to get into his mind. He influenced me by allowing me to influence him. Of course, I did not meet Gandhi in my life. He died two years before I was born, and so that possibility did not exist. But I met him through the son of Mahadev Desai, Narayanbhai Desai. I also met him through dozens of pale imitations. And I kept meeting him in tiny villages and far-flung hills, in remote camps of nomadic communities, in Laxman's cartoons, at railway stations, in obscure schools and places that made the ordinariness of life the heart of its beauty and grandeur.

One day before Narayanbhai passed away, leaving us bereft, a press reporter had come to interview me about my likes and dislikes. When he asked me, 'Who is the one living person in the world that you find worth respecting?' I had immediately responded, 'Narayanbhai Desai'. When the reporter asked me, 'Why?' I had said, 'Because there is no gap between his words and his actions'. This interview appeared in the Gujarati daily *Divya Bhaskar* on the morning of the day that Narayanbhai breathed his last. I know he is no more, but my mind refuses to accept it. Much as I tried to go to Vedchhi for his last rites, and later to the condolence meeting organised in Baroda, I did not have the courage to accept his departure.

Then, there is another window to my memory-hall. When it opened, I was not surprised that it was there at all. It was as if the window was always there and when opened for the first time, it seemed as if it had been opened many times before. This one has neither a past nor a present—it hangs on no hinge. When I look at myself through that window, I find so many others in me and myself in so many others. It is as if a vast thought engulfs us all, passes through all of us, allows us to have its glimpses and offers the possibility of one's learning the humility to accept that the self is but a temporary mark in the ever-flowing stream of some energy, some wisdom. The greater the humility, the clearer is the view of that stream.

The Mahatma attempted many impossible tasks in his life. The most impossible among them was the possibility of crafting an *auto*biography, for that is the worst of the wounds inflicted on truth. I think the very best one can do without being violent to truth is a para-biography.

16 Kolhapur

As you approach this city by train or bus, the sprawling farmlands extended over an unending distance give you a sense of having entered a different space, a sort of a state by itself. Kolhapur was, indeed, a state during the pre-British era, and it has never ever forgotten that it reflected the glory of the Maratha Empire of the eighteenth century. The way the dominant classes speak, think, act, eat, sit, meet and aspire in this city clearly shows a self-consciousness about being in power until just the other day.

That day was about a century and a half gone when I first entered the city. And the moment I got out of the bus, I realised that a misplaced pride was the comic flaw of this place. Throughout the ten years of my stay in this city—years that changed my life altogether—it never once allowed me to forget that I belonged to a caste, that everyone belonged to a caste, and that all other considerations mattered not. Actually, in terms of its demographic makeup, the majority of those who lived there did not belong to the dominant caste. It was just that practically everyone pretended that they did—for not pretending so would have been a crime far more serious. So, deeply put off by the all-pervasive odour of the 'stately caste' I decided to drop the already worn out remnants of my own caste memory, and to pretend the other way round—that I belonged to no caste at all. Strangely, this worked well, much beyond my intentions of stating my difference. The comic flaw was this city knew well how to take pride in one caste and to despise other castes, but it did not have a clue how to react to a casteless individual. Such a person was seen as being exempt from the laws of love and hate, someone welcome everywhere and neither trusted not distrusted. This was a bit like being able to swim freely, but across craggy mountains.

My social life in Kolhapur was unique. Since the city could not place me, it started pleasing me in many ways. Thus, if I wanted to borrow 10 or 20 rupees as loan for an uncertain period, I could ask almost anyone I knew, even a chance acquaintance or the grocer, the laundry man, the unwashed man who ran a little tea-shop. They all normally obliged. I had to of course invent a particular tone and style of Marathi that the Marathi speakers in this city were not used to. They soon learnt to let me live, and I learnt equally soon to live in this city. Though I had not inherited any great social status, I started feeling like a prince. My expressions and my body language changed quite noticeably. I knew that I was being noticed in whatever I did. And I played the role that this city assigned me.

I was here as a student. The university campus was lovely. The buildings, being very new, were all well-painted and well-maintained. The trees planted along the pathways were watered regularly and the flowering plants were kept trimmed. The university had a huge campus, and a lot of the land was still unutilised and covered with tall grasses. When it dried up in the summers, the grass would turn golden in the light of the late afternoon sun. The land was undulating and as there weren't too many tall buildings in the city, the eye could touch the distant horizons unhindered, watch the changing hues of the sky, the shifting clouds, particularly the long and lingering riot of colours at sunset.

A perennial river flowed by the side of the city. On the other side of the river, towards the west, was a historically important fort built during medieval times, now used as a location for shooting Marathi films and a spot for Sunday picnics. Beyond the fort began the foothills of the Sahyadri, beyond which stretched the Arabian Sea, and beyond it the continent called Africa.

This side of the river, there were narrow streets and a marvelous eleventh-century temple built of solid black rock and made of pillars, arches and domes that humans can build only once in a millennium. And straight opposite the temple—one short street away—was a vast lake, made photo-perfect by the majestic walkway all along its margin, and a very real palace built at the beginning of the twentieth century, built because the royal family of Kolhapur and the royal family of Baroda were getting united through a marriage and there was a lovely palace in Baroda but no comparable palace here. So the palace was created.

The city did not know in the past how to cope with outsiders. And it was natural that it did not know how to cope with itself. Hence, despite being one of the most uniquely beautiful cities, the people here just did not know that it was beautiful. Being confused, amnesiac and clueless, they shouted meaninglessly at each other. But there was rarely any menace or violence in the shouting. Even the most polite and friendly greeting here was, 'Hey, you bastard...' And even the worst fights, filled with hatred and loathing, were conducted with the natural patience of *kusti* or wrestling, an important and popular sport here. The city had several grounds for wrestling contests.

Kolhapur also had a great sense of hospitality towards *tamasha* and itinerant street performances. Music and theatre were in every street and corner. Once, 15 years later, when I was at New Haven serving a fellowship sentence in an intellectual den called Yale, a world-famous intellectual had pointed to a street and said to me, 'Here, every foot has an unwritten book'. And in my mind, I thought of Kolhapur—there, every street was a song and a play; how beautiful. That is to say, no one is greatly proud of Kolhapur when one lives there, but no one can ever forget the city when one leaves it. It is almost life. Life that you want to have more of, because nothing you have experienced so far was good enough.

Between the campus and the river is a universe unto itself which is not comparable with any other city in India or outside. Perhaps, Lucknow is the closest trope for it. But Kolhapur has never entertained the desire to cultivate the seeming grace and vivacious courtesy of Lucknow. Drinking? Yes of course, and worse.

In ancient times whenever Kolhapur was struck upon in these enticing hills as a potential site of human habitation, and whoever chanced upon the idea, the overwhelming thought in the mind was of a rock sculpture. Everything here has the attributes of solid black rock and whatever is done in this celestial place has the palpable visibility of a rock. For instance, a simple conversation between two brothers cannot be complete unless a string of the choicest abuses is uttered. A housewife talking to another can open the conversation on the rising prices of coriander by shoving an array of animal genitals up the arse of the government. Help from camels, bullocks, dogs, buffaloes, elephants, donkeys and several protagonists from zoology textbooks is enlisted to serve the point. This must be done in order to make even the simplest communication, no matter what the objects invoked. They can include machines like bulldozers, teaching aids like blackboards, medical instruments like stethoscopes, vehicles like trucks, natural places like hills and mountains, legal documents like electricity bills and court notices, household goods like brooms and almost anything and everything. In Kolhapur, conversations just cannot be completed unless a total organic unity is established between humans and material objects. No, it is not a sex-starved place. It is just a place obsessed with the idea of making sex most graphic.

There is rarely any pornography sold on the pavements and by-lanes of Kolhapur. It has, rather, throngs of prostitutes roaming the streets. You can expect them to be there as naturally as you expect vegetable vendors in Ahmedabad. When a young man is planning to walk down the street to see his fancied girl, practically every other young man in his neighbourhood shouts at him unambiguous advice on how and what precisely he should do, how passionately, how deep and for how long. This neither shames those who happen to hear this, nor the young men who, in another city, would have reason to get enraged. This is normal in Kolhapur, in this city trying to be a sculpted rock.

Another normal thing is the god-man. The city is filled to the brim with god-men and god-women. In my ten years of stay there, I came across many. I came to know of a woman who could see your future lives the moment she cast her eyes on you. I also heard about a young sanyasi—whose younger brother was studying with me—touted as being brighter than Swami Vivekanand. He had a large following of young female devotees. And if any visitor ever criticised him or questioned his spiritual prowess, the person was immediately beaten to a pulp. Then one day, I was invited to ride on my Lambretta scooter to a nearby hill where a yogi sat inside a hole-like cave for six months every year without food, water or air, and still looked alive and charming like a Hindi film actor.

There was a 'spirituality centre' in the city run by the principal of a local college. He had displayed very large and enticing photographs of a contemporary saint. The saint himself lived in a hermitage some 200 kilometres away. This centre did the work of promoting the saint's philosophy of the soul. The spirituality centre was on the first floor of a building. The ground floor of the same building was rented out to several shoe shops, leather work being one of the main industries of Kolhapur. I visited the centre and conversed with the principal several times. My main interest was to get an opportunity of conversing in English, which he could do well. Despite my several visits and conversations, I could not see what was spiritual about the man, either the promoter or the promoted. However, in the process I made a number of friends among the shoe-sellers. This proved very useful as, much later, I decided to gift friends and visitors with Kolhapuri chappals as an ethnic and fancy gift. I got them pretty cheap.

Once, a rather grim-looking man landed in my house. He had arrived from Mysore and his name was something like Krishnamoorthy or Anandamoorthy. He wanted to speak to a group of people in Kolhapur which, I was told, had formed a 'Theosophy Lodge'. He stayed with us for three days, and in those three days I learnt a lot about the 'Elders' and 'Ancients' and 'para-psychology'. He left, leaving on my mind an impression of compassionate humour.

The university stood as an anomaly on the margins of such intense god-pursuit and word-violence. The librarian there was a kind man. He spoke a heavily Kannada-inflected Marathi—quite comic to my ears—and was given to drinking every evening, but he had a discerning eye. When he realised that I was fascinated by books, he allowed me to occupy one of the cubicles that were normally reserved for the faculty. I was allowed to gather all the books of my interest from the shelves and stock them in my cubicle. Besides, the librarian even gave me the permission to spend nights inside the library. This was an unusual arrangement. But I found it immensely useful as I could prepare for my M.A. examinations in a single year while the normal practice was to spend two years. This also reduced for me the drudgery of having to sit in uninteresting lectures by faculty that had no particular grounding in British history or literature. It was much better to read directly from the books rather than be guided by poorly made notes from the very same books and presented to students as lectures. Not that I was particularly bright. It is just that almost everyone else—with a few exceptions—was so terrified of anything English, be it literature, history or books.

This being the case, I stumbled effortlessly through the years from an M.A. to a Ph.D. and from being a reluctant backbencher to a lecturer at the university. Of course, along the way many things happened. I discovered love. I learnt what learning can be. I found out about the larger world. I made lasting friendships with many, including poets, singers, painters, Marxists, businessmen, social creatures, farmers and working-class people. Of these one was a writer of remarkable stature in Kannada. He was also my research supervisor and he left such a deep impression on my thinking and behaviour that I often forget to remember him. My gratitude to him always remains unstated, for it is safer that way.

It was also in Kolhapur that I met Surekha and it was here that a daughter entered our life—a celestial beauty and celestial joy! And it was in Kolhapur that we developed a craze for ice-cream and for old theatre and film songs. It was also here that we learnt for the first time the beauty of risking safety and stability and moving out to unknown worlds. This last was the cementing bond between us.

17 Finding Myself Again and Freedom

When I learnt that I was being given a fellowship to go to the University of Leeds, I thought I was going to be without this unnecessary cultural baggage. However, the result of my moving to England turned out to be the exact opposite of what I had expected it to be. After going to Leeds, I started thinking of myself as being an Indian much more acutely than ever before, and in the process of self-reflection, started thinking of the cultural mix that had formed my personality very intensely. The material arrangements in England are such that the stay there leaves a lot more free time to anyone than the life in India allows. As such, one tends to think about oneself a lot more obsessively. I have noticed that the ego-centrism encouraged by the British lifestyle even makes a person stutter instead of being able to produce simple rapid-fire sentences. For my dissertation at the University of Leeds, I chose to work on two Indian poets who had faced a similar situation, namely R. Parthasarathy and A. K. Ramanujan.

On returning from England, I landed a teaching job in Baroda. Here I came in contact with an eminent Gujarati writer who was a Brahmin, and quite comfortable in the knowledge of being one. He was known in Gujarat as a great modernist writer and thinker. I was quite surprised therefore to see how comfortably he could combine in his sensibility the Sanskrit cultural inheritance and modern Western learning. I observed him with utmost care that combined affection as well as scrutiny. We worked together on a literary journal for five years. When he died, I was getting ready to go to England again. This time, I thought I will make the personality of this great Gujarati writer the subject of my thinking and study. The result of my reflection was a critical book in which I had argued that the contemporary literary sensibility in India suffered by being burdened with the restricting inheritance of Sanskrit theoretical thinking as well as modern forms of Western knowledge. The study was quite esoteric in nature. It was published under the title *After Amnesia*. That it was fairly well received confirmed my suspicion that in our time, Indian people seemed to be looking for a new path that could take them beyond the familiar debates between Brahmanism and its excluded others. But the writing of that study made me experience a new sense of freedom. I felt spiritually lighter. Besides, during the course of this study, I had started discovering the medieval Bhakti poets. They gave me strength.

However, I did not wish to free myself from the dilemma without once carefully and thoroughly looking at the dichotomy. Therefore, I started reading the *Gita* carefully. It created in me an appetite for studying the Vedic literature. Thus I turned to the *Upanishads*. My reading of W. B. Yeats—he had once tried his hand at translating the *Upanishads* with the help of Sri Purohit Swamy—too, had created a curiosity in my mind about these sacred texts. I read some of them, first in order to enjoy them as philosophical texts, and later as texts describing certain deep spiritual experiences. I found them deeply moving and powerfully instructive. Moreover, they did something very profound to me—they drove the fear of death completely out of my mind. Similarly they also took away the sense of material possession which had thus far marked my thinking. When these two changes occurred in me, I started feeling more human. I was forty at the time. And suddenly it dawned on me that I must preserve this precious new freedom brought to me rather unexpectedly. Going over the years of my life, trying to take a good account of all that I had done and not done thus far, I realised that a cultural identity is only a matter of speech, of a language culture. Thus, the idea of looking at various such cultures took hold of my mind. This happened more as a physical experience than as a mental calculation. And, inevitably, I was drawn to the study of languages of small communities. I decided to create the Bhasha Centre for the purpose of carrying out the scrutiny of my new intellectual persuasions. This led me to spending my days with the Adivasis.

As I started living with them, spending endless hours learning from the Adivasis, I felt that for the first time in my life, I could feel completely free. The dilemmas in my mind slowly started dissolving. My anxiety about my own cultural identity slowly started disappearing. The Adivasis taught me that Brahmanism was not just a form of knowledge—it was also a form of power. I realised that Gautam Buddha had gone through this experience long before my time. His teachings started appealing to me, and I decided that I will formulate a series of lectures addressing the *Upanishads* from the Buddha's perspective. I made three attempts to formulate these lectures; but every time when I had finished the first few, I found that the tussle between Buddhism and Brahmanism in my mind was inconclusive. At one point, I had decided to formally convert to Buddhism; but since my mind did not offer a conclusive judgement in the matter, I kept postponing the decision.

After spending about ten years in this state of indeterminacy, one day I took my pen and started writing my last testament. I found myself writing the following sentences which apparently had nothing to do with my material possessions:

> *I would like my body neither to be burnt nor buried. I would like it to be left in water. I have followed a religion with only two articles of faith: one, the world continues even after an individual is no more, and two, the people's wisdom is worth emulating.*

I found it somewhat strange that I should be defining my cultural identity through these articles of faith. Now, all those completely unnecessary debates about my caste and religion that bothered me for half a century have disappeared from my mental transactions. I am free; neither pretending to be a Brahmin, nor any other that survives by hating the Brahmin. I am an Adivasi, I have been here all along, and will be here as long as this earth and the human species continue to be here. I am a thought, only a thought. I will not be reborn for I will never die.

At the heart of that thought is an emptiness that I have been trying to understand for over half a century. Action, excitement, movement, ideals, success, failures, tears, emotions, dreams and fears try to fill that emptiness momentarily. Then it returns again to assuage, to pacify, to temper down, to console, to terrify, to unnerve. It meets you at every corner of life, in crowded streets, in hectic activity, in excited thought, in lonely books, in ancient meditations and in contemporary movies. It is everywhere. I mean everywhere is it. All that is seen and done and thought is but a loss of the memory of this emptiness, the presence of this absence being there all the time and beyond.

I think I had been searching for a while for this little forgetfulness that makes what we call life.

This started with some of my conversations with an elderly Gujarati writer friend, with whom I had been working on the translation journal mentioned before. At that stage I was obsessed with the idea of translating the consciousness of the civilisation that expresses itself in many tongues. Our conversations were not about translation; that was taken for granted in our discussions. They were more about expression—particularly the epic tenor of a lyric expression—and also the agency that allows the expression, the consciousness of it. We were debating—with and through phenomenology and the critics of consciousness—if existence was not but a fiction created by consciousness. These discussions rarely referred to the daily bread and sweat, to the tripping power supply or the communal violence that had become the order of the day. And I must say I remorselessly enjoyed these conversations.

My elderly collaborator and mentor, Suresh Joshi, died within a few years after we launched our conversation. The pain was not so much the loss of his mind for he had shared richly and generously of himself with me; I knew the thought he embodied. The pain for me was knowing that he would not return. I rarely spoke or expressed my emotions, and so I decided to put them in an essay for which I had chosen a most unattractive theme. There was no chance, I imagined, that anybody would ever read it. Perhaps, in an unconscious way, I even tried to make it as unreadable as possible by writing on cultural traditions in two Indian languages in a third non-Indian language using a difficult style, diacritical marks and a tone that was unfriendly from the first sentence to the last. This was my way of meditating on the forgetfulness of the paradoxical emptiness that is everyday life.

18 Baroda[*]

Everything that happens here is on the scale of an epidemic. When children get on the rooftops and balconies to fly kites, they emerge in the thousands and not a dot in the sky is left free for the crows to pass through. As women and men dance through the nine-night Navratri festival, a couple of million feet lift and fall together, step by step. If the city government decides to repair broken roads, several hundred streets get scrubbed and dug up all together and lie in that wounded state for weeks or months. If school children get into the artistic mood, they get together in the thousands to make paintings several kilometres long. The city is already in the *Guinness Book of World Records* for this. If visitors come to the city during the gentle winter months, they come in bus-loads and plane-loads, followed by other train-loads and plane-loads, followed by yet others. In Baroda nothing ever happens quietly and in a small way.

* Author's note: An earlier version of this piece was published as 'Baroda: What a City!', in 'Postcolonial Cities: South Asia', *Moving Worlds: A Journal of Transcultural Writings* 13(2): 24–34, 2013. It is reproduced here with edits, with kind permission of Shirley Chew, and *Moving Worlds*.

Things do happen suddenly. It is not as if the city has no art of springing surprises. But the shock and the surprise have a character all their own. For instance, you think you will surprise your friends by breaking the news of having moved into a new flat. As you extend the paper slip on which you have scribbled the new address, inviting them to the weekend party for your house warming, your friend says, 'In that case we will have lunch at *my* new house. We, too, moved house last week.' Soon, you discover that within a few months all your friends, old and new, have changed their addresses. When a new restaurant opens in this city, practically everybody provides it patronage for the first few weeks. After that the crowds become thinner and the place soon wears a forlorn look.

Everything in this city must happen in the manner of an epidemic. The trees and animals and even the birds know this. The city has a river running through it. We call it a river, though its width is so slight that a first-time visitor could easily mistake it for a drainage canal. In this ribbon of a river, crocodiles arrive from water bodies afar, not two or three but several dozen. If one were to walk over their backs, there would be no need of a bridge over the river. The crocodile density, too, has earned this city a place in books of world records. Likewise, when parrots alight on trees in Baroda, they alight in the thousands. What is surprising, though, is that these green singers are quite 'post-colonial' in their entire behaviour. This needs some explaining.

The old city lies on one side of the river; the cantonment that the colonial Resident Officer ordered into existence is on the other side of the crocodile-infested river. The railway tracks that arrived half a century after the British officers did were laid in such a way that both the city and the cantonment had an easy access to the railway station. The 'civil lines', the polite colonial expression for the 'torture machine' constituted by various commanding officers, were laid way beyond the railway station.

The bungalows here are palatial with large rooms and high roofs, surrounded by open spaces for pets and servant quarters, and unusually high compound walls.

The residents of Baroda rarely ventured out to this area. They occasionally saw the mounted guards emerging from there for the night patrol. Even after Independence, citizens felt uneasy if they were required to go beyond the railway station. Senior government officers occupied the bungalows vacated by the British administrators. Sometime in the early 1970s, parrots started making the trees in this area their overnight nesting place. And by the mid-1970s, when Baroda came into the national news for what is known as 'the dynamite case', two trees next to the police commissioner's bungalow were completely colonised by parrots from north and south, east and west. They came in the thousands, and while their manners were entirely native, they made themselves comfortable on those two neem and banyan trees. An epidemic of parrots, what else?

First, the bird droppings made the black tar road chalk white. Add to that the generous sprinkling of *paan* spit, and the white continents grew neat little red islands. The noisy tumult of the parrots could be heard for kilometres around every evening and morning. Citizens started thronging to watch them as they alighted on the trees at sunset every evening. Following the bird watchers, the peanut vendors and the *paani-puri* stalls arrived. Then gradually, throwaway pornography books and old American fiction showed up along the pavements, sold at 'one rupee an item'. A few weeks later, an enterprising cane-furniture maker placed a few of his inexpensive cane book shelves and chairs for sale on the pavement opposite the peanut vendor.

In due time, the mint sellers, the fortune tellers, the garment repairers, the lock and key makers, the rubber stamp vendors started showing up. A few flower girls started selling tiny jasmine *maalas* for women's ponytails. A rather taciturn man brought stamp-sized coloured pictures of Hindu gods, freedom fighters, cricket celebrities, Abraham Lincoln and Mother Teresa to liven up the emerging market. Soon arrived the calendar seller whose prints of Bombay cinema actresses quickly became bestsellers. These silent mutinies collectively created a bazaar. And as every Indian bazaar does, it stamped the entire area with a character uniquely that of a bazaar. It was around this time that I arrived in Baroda. And I have seen over the last four decades the colonial memories wiped out bit by bit every day. Today, the parrots have gone. And the bazaar has grown into an imposing street lined with malls.

The street was first named after a colonial administrator Romesh Chunder Dutt, appointed by the Rajah of Baroda, a poet and a historian. The street name was first reduced to his initials as R. C. Dutt Street. Gradually, as the malls came up on it, the street name was forgotten. Today, it is known more in terms of the multi-storeyed buildings and shopping complexes such as 'The Panorama' or 'The Alkapuri Arcade'. The malls, too, have come up on a scale that is typical of Baroda. The peanuts, calendars, cane chairs and the stamp-sized gods have all gone.

I have jumped forward. I should first tell you about my parrot. This one was one of those thousands in the Alkapuri 'civil lines' zone. I spotted it outside the university campus. The university campus and the railway station in Baroda are built next to each other as, long ago, students and scholars from all parts of India used to go to Baroda for studying at the Maharaja Sayajirao University. When the city started growing beyond its initial aspirations, the railway station became a favourite place for the homeless. During the day time, they generally loitered around the station area. The university campus had some open spaces, and the large public park on the other side of the campus had even more space. These spaces became useful. The more enterprising among the loiterers set up small and big ventures, which would run for a few days, until the police whisked them away or confiscated their petty goods and belongings. One such venture appeared on the pavement outside the compound wall of the majestic Arts Faculty building. A man sat on the ground with a few homemade cards laden with graffiti that we were supposed to take for Tibetan or some such esoteric script. Next to him, in a cubical wooden cage, sat a parrot trained to pick up these cards. This parrot had all the knowledge, a lot more than the university on the other side of the wall could ever store in its library. You approached the man, sat down in front of the cage, shyly stated your problem or asked a question in your mind, and looked at the parrot for the right answer. And, lo and behold, the parrot picked up a card from the lot presented to it, or at least touched one with its sad red beak. That card contained the answer to your question, and the man would read it out from the esoteric script for your benefit. You paid him the fees, a rupee or two at the most, and left after thanking the parrot in amazement.

I had recently joined the university, and as I strolled to the Bank of Baroda or the tea shops, I would see this parrot of knowledge. As I had no problems to solve or questions to ask, I did not quite go up to the fellow; but occasionally, I did offer the man some small money for buying an umbrella or a shirt. Before you knew it, more such divine men and parrots started squatting along the compound wall. The numbers multiplied. This was, in a way, knowledge in a competitive market. I was getting curious about the increasing numbers and so decided to quiz the original parrot man. 'Why do you continue with these petty deceptions?' I asked him. 'No sir,' he said, unfazed by my superior moral stand. 'Many come to me from the university. Some have listened to the Parrot Maharaja's advice and set up tuition classes. They have prospered. Three girls got married to green-card holders and are already in America. Many come. They get wise answers...' The green cards! I noticed that this fellow had the acumen of a psychiatrist to have combined the green of the parrot and the cards that it picked up. This was also the time when the green-card epidemic had started hitting Baroda. Inside my classroom, students were no longer interested in learning literary styles and political philosophies. They were interested in acquiring a few English words, just enough to enable them to stand behind the counters in a Liverpool or a New Jersey corner shop. I knew then that the parrot man knew the city better than I did. This recognition made us friends. He told me that this city has not only the parrot people but also the elephant people. By the time I could get to the elephant people, and without much effort, the university made me a reader, and then a professor. But I was not the only one. The university positions, too, came on a scale that is typical of this place.

The elephant people! These are tiny men and women, rarely over five feet three inches, and quite bulky, the bulk makes them appear even shorter. Their livelihood is a complicated business. Early in the morning they hire an elephant at 80 rupees an hour. All of them dress in home-dyed maroon. Three men walk in front of the elephant. Two walk at the back. The owner sits atop. One man walks alongside the elephant. This one is normally the oldest of the lot, with a long beard and long hair. He does not speak. The ones who walk ahead make the elephant stop every few yards. Then they shout loud enough so the entire neighbourhood can hear: 'The Swami has returned from the Himalayas after 12 years of meditation. He will not speak for the next 28 years. Come and take his blessings.' The elephant procession easily lends credence to the claim. People step out and bow down to the silent one. They offer gifts. He does not accept any. The people in the front scold them, 'Do you not know that he has given up everything? He will not even touch a gift. He can make the universe dance at his will. How dare you offer gifts to him? Who do you think you are, king or god?' The givers feel ashamed and plead with the followers of the 'saint' to accept at least something. They condescend and say that gifts may be given only to the elephant. But what can be given to an elephant? So, people bring out bags filled with rice and wheat and sugar and tins of oil and stuff like that. Now you cannot really offer an elephant just a couple of bananas or a stale half-sandwich. The quantities must be large. Large quantities indeed are collected. The show is repeated every few hundred yards, for over a few hours. Then the performers vanish, apparently for their journey back to the Himalayas. The large collection is distributed evenly among these people. The elephant rentals are paid. The next day the show moves to another locality.

The community engaged in this occupation is called Davre Gosavi. They were wrongly victimised during the colonial rule and declared as a 'criminal tribe'. In the lean season, the Davre Gosavis send their women to stand outside temples with rented cows. Another group of their women stands close by, selling green fodder. As the devotees are about to enter the temple the cow-keepers call out for offerings to the cows. Cows are sacred here, particularly in the mornings. In the evenings, they may appear in clandestine restaurants as appetising dishes. But mornings are mornings after all. The devotees buy fodder off the women and offer it to the cow-keeping women. The same fodder is recycled and sold over and over again till it is lunch time. Finally, the cows get it. The women go home with the proceeds and have their lunch. While the women are at work outside temples, the men among the Davre Gosavis play cards, drink and dream of a better tomorrow. I was initially interested in the parrot people, the elephant men and the cow women as I found close similarities between their work and my work inside the university. But over the years, my interest grew beyond self-accusation. I noticed that they were not alone. Communities and localities like theirs were tucked behind every main street.

Baroda has numerous majestic buildings. Maharaja Sayajirao Gaekwad of Baroda—beginning his greatly benevolent rule in the last quarter of the nineteenth century and remaining at the helm for a good four decades of the twentieth century—had turned Baroda from a sleepy little town to a remarkable capital of the most progressive state in India. He wanted to build Baroda to vie with Edinburgh, and the university here to compete with Cambridge. The marvelous red brick buildings with minarets and domes are a testimony to the king's grand dream. He created the colleges, courts, palaces, lovely bungalows, offices, markets, lakes, music and theatre places, museums and parks—all located in spacious plots with plenty of trees. In his six decades of rule, the Maharaja turned Baroda into an architectural marvel.

There were people, however, residing in the erstwhile Baroda town. They belonged to different communities who had come to Baroda for different reasons at different points in time. The Muslim community emerged because the previous ruler, not quite of Baroda but of neighbouring Champaner, happened to be a Muslim. The Marathas came with the Maratha chieftains, and they stayed since the Maharaja himself was from a Marathi-speaking community. The Gujarati merchants made Baroda their home as their business flourished without the risks of abrupt confiscation of their properties. The others made it their home as their craft and skills were in demand. The communities mostly lived in their own separate localities, not quite ghettoes but sufficiently pronounced in the specific caste, religion and language identities.

The Maharaja was busy throughout his life in creating a contemporary idiom in administration, architecture and the arts. Hence the boulevards, the lakes, the majestic buildings came up; but the different communities continued to live in segregation. And the communities that lived by their craft and skills suffered the most with every economic transition. The Maharaja left such a strong legacy of his vision of the city that all those who followed thereafter could barely change its character. Neither could they weld together the growth of the city with the growth of its many communities. Go anywhere in Baroda and you find at least something named after the Maharaja. Thus the general hospital is called Sayaji Hospital. The university is Sayajirao University. The most frequented public park is the Sayaji Garden. The area that you first encounter after arriving in the city is Sayaji Gunj. As an extension of this statement of gratitude, Baroda has named many of its other public places after the close relatives of the Maharaja. A great soul, greatly remembered.

But the communities continued to exist with their late medieval legacy. And the ones who lost their livelihood as the economy turned new corners came to be tucked away invisibly in localities that are a little further from the boulevards and the majestic buildings. These are the parrot people, the elephant people, the cow people. And little was done in Baroda to work out a social harmony that included them. Sad but true.

The man who brought the most progressive legislation to India after Independence was once a poor student seeking help for his studies. Maharaja Sayajirao gave him that help. Financial assistance from the Maharaja took Babasaheb Ambedkar, an 'untouchable boy', to the University of Columbia for an M.Sc. in Political Science and a Ph.D. When the scholarship ended, out of his sense of gratitude for Sayajirao, Babasaheb decided to work in the Baroda State Service where he was offered the position of Political Secretary to the Maharaja. The Maharaja had always tried to attract brilliant Indians from various walks of life to Baroda in an attempt to create a model progressive state. Two decades before Ambedkar joined the Baroda State Service, Sayajirao Gaekwad had brought another illustrious son of India to Baroda. This was Aurobindo Ghosh, who was called from Cambridge to work as Sayajirao's Secretary. But, while Sri Aurobindo worked in Baroda for nearly two decades, Dr. Ambedkar's stay did not last even two weeks. For one thing, nobody received him on arrival at Baroda, and his assistants were reluctant to take orders from him at the work place. Far worse was the fact that while waiting to get the official bungalow it became impossible for him to find even a simple accommodation in Baroda.

On reaching Baroda, Ambedkar started wondering which hotel would accept him. In those days, there were inns in Baroda where travellers and visitors used to stay. Alternately, there was the state guest house. Ambedkar felt that Hindu inns would surely refuse to take him in. Therefore, he decided to try some Parsi inn, but he soon discovered that these, too, were meant only for Parsis. Having no choice, he had to plead with the owner of a Parsi inn to allow him to stay there on condition of secrecy so that other Parsis did not ostracise the inn owner. Ambedkar knew that this was but a temporary difficulty as he was hoping to get the official bungalow as per his entitlement. Little did he know that his stay at the Parsi inn would be very short, and that it would end tragically. The place was not really fit for a person of his position. On the eleventh day of this kind of strange and despicable arrangement, he was indeed spotted by other members of the Parsi community and was unceremoniously served marching orders. The humiliation and the agony were too much for Dr. Ambedkar to bear any longer; and that night he took the 9 p.m. train back to Bombay, never to return to Baroda.

I had heard this story before coming to Baroda in the 1980s. But the appearance of the city is so soothing and the people so gentle that I always thought that the story could not possibly have been true. My scepticism lasted until Habib Tanveer, one of India's legendary greats in theatre, came to Baroda. He was planning to spend a year working on a theatre production with students of the performing arts. I was inducted by mutual friends into finding a suitable house for Tanveer. But a Muslim does not find a house in Baroda easily, except in the Muslim ghettoes. And this Habib Tanveer was not prepared to do. He had spent long years working with the progressive theatre movement and was a vocal atheist and a leftist. So, despite trying with all my friends, acquaintances, estate agents known to me and even all possible strangers, I could not find a house on rent for him. He even tried to find lodgings in a disused cinema studio; the rest of his team was accommodated there, but not him. I then had to accept that what had happened to Dr. Ambedkar as an 'untouchable' was as true as what happened to the Muslim, Habib Tanveer. Baroda has a lot on display, as there is a lot that it hides. This is possibly the only reason why the city has inspired such great imagination and creativity among so many of its inhabitants.

The Baroda artists have always been an enigma to me. The per capita presence of creative artists in this city is easily the highest in India, and should be among some of the highest in the world. If you go out for a stroll from Kala Ghoda, a memorial statue of Sayajirao, to Fatehgunj, it is rare that you do not run into at least a couple of national celebrities in the art world. Painters, sculptors, designers, architects, dancers, musicians, photographers, museum archivists, art collectors, art critics, gallery managers, Baroda has them all.

I had heard of Baroda as a place for the arts and I had heard of the names of some of the great painters of my times as the 'Baroda School' painters. But, through my four decades of stay here, I see no end to the emergence of new talent. For instance, you see someone as an undergraduate student. You lend him some books—knowing they will probably never be returned—scold him a bit about his poor reading or writing skills and soon, all but push him into your passive memory. Some years later you are travelling through London or Paris or Washington, and suddenly the forgotten undergraduate emerges in your view. As you are struggling to figure out where you saw this person the last time and prepare yourself to ask him if he finally landed a job in some IT joint, he will hand you his visiting card and invite you to his 'show'. 'Where?' you ask. And without hesitation he tells you, 'Here, in the National Gallery.' Or the Smithsonian or some such place, places that you normally find quite exotic and prestigious, places where you imagine only the Picassos of the world exhibit. This has happened to me in at least in ten capital cities of the world. But such is Baroda. It keeps producing artist after artist. Quite in tune with the Baroda scale of things. No one has so far figured out the secret of Baroda's tireless burgeoning creativity. Perhaps, the roots are to be found in the challenges thrown up by the huge gap between the visible face of the city and its invisible limbs. You cannot brush aside this gap by using the cliché 'paradox'. The void yawning between the body and the face is far too wide to be described merely as a paradox. It is a perpetual spiritual war that provides the creative passion and energy of epidemic proportions that Baroda brings to everything.

A decade after I settled in this city, I noticed three new horizons opening up in the minds of the younger generation. One was to get away from the city and go off to the US. If you live in Mumbai and ever step out at dawn for your morning walk and happen to walk past the American Consulate, you would see the early signs of a huge queue building up for visa applications. If you were curious to know who these modern-day descendents of Columbus were, you would not have to begin with the first girl or boy in the queue. It would be okay to begin with the sixth, for the first five would invariably be from Baroda. Such was the craze for the American visa.

The second horizon was pharmaceuticals or the chemical industry. Ask every high-school child what she or he wants to do, if they do not end up going to the US. They did not have to think to answer your question, and they would tell you they have already selected a piece of land reserved for industrial units. Five years later, you could easily walk into their offices to collect a good donation for a charity. Boys and girls in Baroda were doing this when the young people in the rest of the country were spending endless years preparing for admission to medical or engineering colleges or getting into the Indian Administrative Services. The university had asked me to run a centre for training undergraduates for the IAS examinations. I tried training over 500; only three of them passed the examination—two were from outside Gujarat. The one from Baroda who decided to join opted for the economic services and went on to become an Income Tax Officer. And as he had a good rank, he insisted on getting the Gujarat state for his posting. He knew where the money was.

The third horizon that unfolded in the imagination of the young during the 1980s was the finance market. If you were having a chat with a helper in the laboratory and if you were to express your concern over the rising prices, take it that you were about to make a deadly mistake. Such ordinary things just did not interest the fellow. Nor would it help if you decided to switch to politics, apartheid, the Arab–Jew conflict, or the newly-circulating terms like 'perestroika' and 'glasnost'. Nothing would wash. But the moment you mentioned the name of a top-class stock or the fluctuation in shares and debentures, his eyes glittered. He would then note down your address, drop in at your place that very evening and persuade you to hand over your financial portfolio to him to handle. Migration to the US, setting up a trading or production unit in chemicals or pharmaceuticals, and getting into the finance market hit Baroda, as everything else, as incurable epidemics. Never mind that it continued to produce artists and writers as before.

The elephant people and the parrot people were neither artists nor money-makers. They were merely there. More such 'merely there' people continued to pour into the city. These came mostly from the eastern tribal districts. First they would come as construction workers. Then they became small-time labour contractors. And finally they just settled into the nooks and crannies of the city. They were everywhere, although they were nowhere. The tension mounted. The ghettoes continued to close in: you for yourselves and us for ourselves; they for themselves and the rest for the others. The unstated tensions kept rising to a boiling point. But it was not on a scorching hot day of the Baroda summer that it suddenly exploded.

The summers in Baroda drive you mad. They will drive anybody mad. No, not for the 40 centigrade plus temperature, but for the riot of colours that washes the city. Baroda knows well how to beat the scorching sun. The raw mango *sharbat* and the cool buttermilk consumed in generous doses take care of the heat outside. Besides, as you step inside a house or an office, a cool glass of water is offered to you. It is the sudden summer fury of laburnums that drives you mad. The laburnum blossom is such a flamboyant yellow that you cannot think of anything else once you have glanced at the branches heavy with flowers. I cannot describe the glory of these fantastic trees except by saying fancifully that if it took a five feet seven inches tall William Wordsworth to dance with joy in the company of daffodils, it will take a hundred and fifty-seven feet tall poet to convey just how mesmerising the laburnums are. A. K. Ramanujan, a poet who lived here briefly, tried his hand at this. All he could do was to contrast the 'yellow upon yellow' blossoms with the heavy feet of a prisoner just out of the Central Jail. But he achieved nothing more than to indicate the correct postal address of a row of Baroda laburnums. For indeed the Jail Road is lined with laburnums. Summers in Baroda are a time of wordless admiration and quiet withdrawal nurtured by *lassi* and *sharbat*.

It is the winters that thrill Baroda. Once the monsoon ends, mostly after an indifferent spell, come the festivals, the conferences, the concerts, the friends and homecomings, the book releases and art exhibitions, the marathons and charity shows, the designer garment sales and craft bazaars. It is in winter that all the public events in Baroda happen. The elections, scandals, murders at the railway station, collection of extortion money, buying and selling of residential properties, divorces, dances and dinner parties at the farm houses, all these are the winter events of Baroda. In 2002, the winter in Baroda brought riots. Real riots. Mostly Muslims, and in a few cases Hindus, were slaughtered. Houses were set on fire. Vehicles were smashed. Women were raped publicly. The face and the limbs of Baroda tried for one last desperate time to free themselves from each other. The ghettoes tightened themselves and clashed with other ghettoes, causing blood baths. The creative imagination fainted. Decency and humanity took a month-long holiday. And unprecedented figures were added to the record book of crime.

This one time, one had to look down in shame for being in Baroda. Individuals repented after the riots subsided. The city showed no remorse, though. The parrots did not home in at the famous trees that year. They no longer do. The artists lived in terror for a decade following the riots and took their work to other cities. In Baroda they mutely decided to become faceless. The elephant people stopped their processions and the cow women stopped frequenting the temples. The finance market men continued with their business as usual and did even better perhaps. The pharmaceuticals prospered. After the silence caused by the shock of the brutality, there were no voices heard in Baroda. Then one fine morning, we saw posters proclaiming the unbelievable progress of Baroda put up everywhere. The posters changed, the theme did not. The posters displayed the photographs, in many different poses, of someone who had encouraged the riots, but always with the same remorseless face. The posters, too, came to Baroda on a scale that cannot be described by any lesser an epithet than 'epidemic'. What a city!

19 A Search for Completion

Every time I have moved into a new city, it has primarily been moving into a new dwelling. The houses that I moved into in different cities were either better than the other houses there, or worse than them. They were never just houses by themselves. Moving into a new city was always moving into a new competitive space. In those houses, there were things that were necessary to make life possible, and I did not make any of those by myself. The shapes and sizes, the textures and styles, the functions and utility of those things were all designed by other people, elsewhere. I merely found myself surrounded by those objects, with my existence incomplete without them. Thus, moving into a new city was always moving into the time and space made by others. In a way, this was to remain an unfinished, incomplete being. No, not my mind, which was complete in itself. Which brought with it to each new city layers of memory, the memory of many times. But the space remained the same. It was the space that plunged me into a contested zone where I arrived only to realise how incomplete I was. This was always a sure recipe for feeling alienated. In that alienation, I was a beast of burden carrying many times in my memory, and carrying them into the same space. So many cities passed through my life, but the space I found in them was the same.

I could escape that space only if I entered the crevices of those cities, found the forgotten people, entered their consciousness and started looking at the world through their eyes. When that happened, I could find myself, could feel a little less unfinished, a little less incomplete, in more of a continuum with the rest and not broken away from them. The Bhois in Bhor, the elephant people in Baroda, the Gypsies in Leeds, and the Kanjar-bhats in Kolhapur were all such people who joined for me one layer of time in my mind with other scattered layers of time, expanded my space confined to my cluttered dwellings out towards those wandering feet in the streets. When that happened, I thought, at least momentarily, the space and time in which I lived had become one, neither retaining their identity; together they were my 'spots of time', allowing me to see myself in the mirror of the world around me. At all other times and in all other places, I was blinded by the distance between my space and my time.

During the years I studied in college and university, my exposure to the academic discipline called psychology was fairly limited. My impressions of the mind were guided by the limited experience of my own sentiments. The terminology I had at my disposal for any possible understanding of the inner workings of my mind was drawn from popular theology. For instance, there was some discussion about the workings of the consciousness, or mind, in parts of the *Bhagwad Gita* that I had crammed during my school days. Besides, the rich stock of stories I had read had narratives of *par-kaya pravesh*, getting under another person's skin, of the mind changing bodies and the body changing minds, and such transmigrational fantasy. There were also stories from the *Mahabharata* depicting a disembodied mind residing deep in a well. All of these had assembled in my mind as a mangled wealth of heritage and insight.

When I was 21, I noticed an advertisement in the *Reader's Digest* announcing a discount on very beautifully produced and bound classics under the imprint of *Everyman's Library*. I had no money to procure the volumes, but after working towards collecting the necessary amount, I gathered the courage to stake my hard-earned money. In good time the books were delivered to me, all of them with golden embroidered edges. They included a Plato, a Kafka, a Darwin and a Freud. The last among these was an entity till then unknown to me. Therefore, I made it a priority to read it first. The analysis of dreams in it was so fresh for me that I decided to read the volume to the last page. A few years later I came across an analysis of some of the stream of consciousness writers like James Joyce and Virginia Woolf; and that opened up for me further paths of getting to know a little more about Freudian psychology. By the time I was 25, I had gathered enough of a general knowledge about Jung and Adler as well. This led to my beginning to describe the mind in terms of the unconscious, ego, neurosis, amnesia and so on. It is common that when one gets hold of a convenient tool to catch something, the dependence on that tool keeps increasing.

It was in my mid-thirties that I started looking again at my looking at the mind and started becoming a bit uneasy about many of the formulations of the early twentieth-century psychology. At this time I was reading a lot about the origin and development of anthropology, and getting acquainted with the skeletons in its cupboard, its colonial roots. A similar view of psychology would have made it appear pure fiction, an imagined narrative deeply rooted in its own period and influenced by the politics of the day. In this case, it would be the politics of race and gender.

Later still, as I started working with nomadic communities and the indigenous Adivasis, and as my interest in looking at everything entirely as a consequence of colonialism had faded, I could free myself of the anxiety for psychology's origin. Later still, when I turned to the study of the language diversity in India, the interest in neurology helped me to understand the nature of what we describe as 'mental' transactions. It was as if the mind is a narrative, and neural circuits the typewriter with which this narrative is scripted. I am sure that if I were to continue chasing the matter, my understanding will shift again. But as of now, and from where I am, the mind appears to be no more than the body. Hence, the question of a 'disembodied mind' is like the question of a tune without melody.

The random account of my growth and progression through time that I have attempted to present in the earlier sections is an attempt to say why I think Time exists not unless it is within space, and why the mind exists not unless it is very much of the body. Life has been a process of discovering the space and the body which often get mistaken as time and mind. Many mighty thinkers and poets have attempted to write their autobiographies in the manner of a history of ideas, as a story of the growth of their minds. In my case, the story is much simpler. It says that both the idea of growth and the idea of mind are no more than imagined narratives. One can tell a story of 'things'. How can one tell a story of a story? I have now realised that what I seek to know is much farther than I had imagined it to be when I first set out to know it. I realise that it is just not there. How can I not cry out in shock that it is not there! That it cannot be known. That it can be experienced but not 'known'. I can no longer remain silent about this. Can anyone human?